# PIES
## and
# CAKES

Better Homes and Gardens

# PIES
# and
# CAKES

**MEREDITH PRESS**
**New York    Des Moines**

# CONTENTS

## PIES

## CAKES

*On our cover:* Cherry-raspberry Pie and Tropical Chiffon Cake.
*Opposite page:* Jelly-glazed Pizza Peach Pie and Banana Cake with Creamy Strawberry Fluff team-up for casual parties.

Our checked seal assures you that every recipe in *Pies and Cakes* is tested and endorsed by the Better Homes and Gardens Test Kitchen. Each recipe is tested until it measures up to the high standards of family appeal, practicality, and deliciousness.

Better Homes TEST KITCHEN

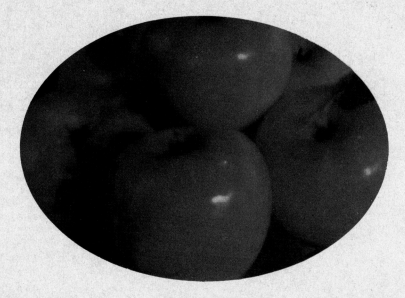

# PERFECT PIES

A man's first choice for dessert? Pie! That's why one of the first baking ventures of a bride is likely to be a pie, and why experienced cooks serve pie for almost every special occasion. And that's why we have devoted the first section of this book to pie recipes. Discover spicy fruit pies, smooth cream pies, cloud-light chiffon, and frosty parfait pies—pies that are standards and favorites with excellent cooks and recipes with a different twist.

Included are many pies which get a head start from convenience foods, cutting pie-making time to minutes. You'll find tips from our test kitchen, too, for making tender, flaky pastry, perfect meringues, and satiny creamy fillings. We suggest trims for picture-pretty pies to please your eye as well as your taste. Each recipe has been carefully tested to insure best results each time it is made.

Simply the World's Greatest Apple Pie! Cut through the basket weave top crust to a spicy-tart fruit filling.

# PERENNIAL FRUIT PIE FAVORITES

## WORLD'S GREATEST APPLE PIE

Pastry for 9-inch lattice-top pie
6 or 7 tart apples, pared, cored, and
thinly sliced (6 cups)
¾ to 1 cup sugar
2 tablespoons all-purpose flour
½ to 1 teaspoon cinnamon
Dash *each* nutmeg and salt
2 tablespoons butter or margarine

If apples lack tartness, sprinkle with 1 tablespoon lemon juice. Combine sugar, flour, cinnamon, nutmeg, and salt; mix with sliced apples. Line 9-inch pie plate with pastry; fill with apple mixture. Dot with butter or margarine.

To make basket lattice top, cut 18 strips ¾-inch wide with pastry wheel. Weave lattice on baking sheet generously sprinkled with sugar. Tilt baking sheet over far edge of filled pie and slide lattice onto filling. Trim and seal edge.

Sprinkle top with sugar. Fold strip of foil or pie tape around rim of crust, covering fluted edge. (This keeps juices in pie and guards against boil-over and overbrowning.) Bake in hot oven (400°) 55 to 60 minutes or till apples are done. Serve pie slightly warm.

*Note:* To save time, two 1-pound 4-ounce cans (about 5 cups) pie-sliced apples, drained, may be substituted for fresh apples.

## 1-2-3 APPLE PIE

1 *baked* 9-inch pastry shell
1 1-pound 5-ounce can French apple
pie filling
¾ cup milk
1 cup dairy sour cream
1 3¾- or 3⅝-ounce package
*instant* vanilla pudding mix
2 tablespoons sliced toasted almonds

Turn pie filling into pastry shell. Slowly add milk to sour cream, mixing well. Add pudding mix and beat according to package directions. Pour pudding mixture over pie filling. Chill. Garnish top with toasted almonds.

## RHUBARB-APPLE PIE

Pastry for 9-inch lattice-top pie
1½ cups sugar
⅓ cup sifted all-purpose flour
½ teaspoon salt
3 cups fresh rhubarb cut in 1-inch
pieces (about ¾ pound)
2 large tart apples, pared, cored, and
sliced (2 cups)
2 tablespoons butter or margarine

Combine sugar, flour, and salt. Toss with rhubarb and apple until mixed well. Let stand 20 minutes. Turn into pastry-lined 9-inch pie plate. Dot with butter. Adjust lattice top; seal. Bake in hot oven (400°) about 55 minutes. Cool.

## APPLE-GO-ROUND PIZZA

*A dessert pizza. Sounds crazy, you say? Try it, we say!—*

Pastry based on 2 cups flour
7 to 8 medium apples, cored and sliced
1½ tablespoons lemon juice
⅓ cup sugar
1 teaspoon cinnamon
¼ teaspoon nutmeg
¾ cup sifted all-purpose flour
½ cup sugar
½ cup butter or margarine

Cut a 15-inch circle of heavy-duty aluminum foil. Roll pastry on foil to fit circle. Trim edge with pastry wheel or knife; place pastry on foil on a large baking sheet.

Beginning ¾ inch from edge of pastry, make circles, one inside the other, of overlapping apple slices. Sprinkle apples with lemon juice. Combine ⅓ cup sugar with spices; sprinkle over apples. Combine flour and ½ cup sugar; cut in butter till crumbly; sprinkle over top.

Turn up the ¾-inch rim of pastry and foil; flute. Bake in very hot oven (450°) 20 to 25 minutes or till crust is brown and apples are tender. Serve warm. Garnish center with wedges of cheese. Makes 10 servings.

## VERMONT APPLE PIE

*A tribute to New England, with real "down East" flavor—*

6 large tart apples, pared, cored, and
   sliced (6 cups)
1 *unbaked* 9-inch pastry shell
⅓ to ½ cup sugar
¾ cup gingersnap crumbs
1 tablespoon all-purpose flour
½ teaspoon cinnamon
Dash salt
¼ cup butter or margarine, melted
¼ cup chopped California walnuts
⅓ cup maple-flavored syrup

Spread *half* the apples in pastry shell. Combine next 6 ingredients; spread *half* the mixture over apples. Spread remaining apples atop first layer; top with remaining crumbs and the walnuts. Bake in moderate oven (375°) about 50 minutes, covering with foil the last 25 minutes. Remove from oven. Pour syrup evenly over pie.

## CARAMEL APPLE PIE

Pastry for 2-crust 9-inch pie
6 to 8 tart apples, pared, cored, and
   sliced
¼ cup granulated sugar
2 tablespoons all-purpose flour
1 teaspoon cinnamon
¼ teaspoon salt
2 tablespoons butter or margarine, melted
⅓ cup dark corn syrup
¼ cup brown sugar
2 tablespoons all-purpose flour
2 tablespoons butter or margarine,
   softened
¼ cup dark corn syrup
¼ cup chopped California walnuts

Arrange apples in pastry-lined 9-inch pie plate. Combine next 6 ingredients; pour over apples. Adjust top crust, cutting slits for escape of steam; seal. Bake in hot oven (425°) 40 minutes or till crust is browned and apples are tender. (Cover rim of crust with foil if it browns too rapidly.) Remove from oven. Combine remaining ingredients except nuts; spread over pie; sprinkle with nuts. Return pie to oven for 5 minutes or till topping is bubbly. (Place baking sheet under pie to catch topping that may run off.)

## BLUEBERRY-APPLE PIE

Pastry for 2-crust 9-inch pie
1 cup sugar
3 tablespoons cornstarch
¼ teaspoon cinnamon
2 cups fresh blueberries *or* 1 10-ounce
   package frozen blueberries, thawed
3 cups pared, cored, sliced tart apples
1 teaspoon lemon juice
2 tablespoons butter or margarine

Combine sugar, cornstarch, cinnamon, and dash salt. Add to blueberries and apples and stir to coat. Turn into pastry-lined 9-inch pie plate. Drizzle with lemon juice; dot with butter. Adjust top crust, cutting slits for escape of steam; seal. Bake at 400° about 50 minutes. Cool.

## SOUR CREAM APPLE PIE

Combine ½ cup granulated sugar, 1 tablespoon all-purpose flour, ¼ teaspoon salt, ¼ teaspoon cinnamon, and ¼ teaspoon nutmeg. Toss with 6 cups pared, cored, sliced tart apples. Arrange in *unbaked* 9-inch pastry shell. Cover loosely with foil. Bake in hot oven (400°) 50 to 55 minutes, or till apples are tender. Remove foil. Combine 1 cup dairy sour cream and ¼ cup brown sugar. Pour evenly over apples. Sprinkle with nutmeg. Bake 2 to 3 minutes longer.

## DEEP DISH APPLE PIE

8 large tart apples, pared, cored, and
   sliced (8 cups)
¾ to 1 cup sugar
1 teaspoon nutmeg
1 tablespoon butter or margarine
Pastry based on 1½ cups flour
Custard Sauce

Place apples in 9x9x2-inch baking dish; top with combined sugar and nutmeg; dot with butter. Roll pastry into a 10-inch square ⅛-inch thick. Place over filling, cutting slits for escape of steam; seal. Bake at 425° about 40 minutes. Serve with *Custard Sauce:* Combine 1 cup light cream, 2 slightly beaten egg yolks, and ¼ cup sugar in double boiler. Cook over hot water, stirring constantly, till mixture coats metal spoon.

## FRENCH CRUNCH PEACH PIE

Drain one 1-pound 13-ounce can sliced peaches well and turn into *unbaked* 9-inch pastry shell. Beat 1 egg slightly; stir in 1 tablespoon lemon juice and ⅓ cup sugar. Pour over peaches. Mix 1 cup (about 24) vanilla-wafer crumbs, ¼ cup butter or margarine, melted, and ½ cup chopped toasted almonds; sprinkle over filling. Bake in hot oven (400°) about 25 minutes or till pastry is browned and filling is set in center. Cool thoroughly before cutting.

## PEACH CARAMEL PIE

Turn one 1-pound 5-ounce can peach pie filling into *unbaked* 9-inch pastry shell. Combine one 7½-ounce package caramel frosting mix (dry) and ½ cup sifted all-purpose flour; cut in 6 tablespoons butter or margarine. Sprinkle over top. Bake at 375° for 40 to 45 minutes.

## BROWN-SUGAR PEACH PIE

*Peaches bake to perfection in a rich caramel sauce—*

Prepare pastry for 9-inch lattice-top pie. Combine ¾ cup brown sugar, ⅓ cup all-purpose flour, 3 tablespoons light corn syrup, 1 tablespoon lemon juice, and ⅓ cup softened butter or margarine. Cook and stir over low heat till sugar is dissolved; cool slightly. Arrange 6 fresh peaches, sliced, *or* 3½ cups well-drained canned sliced peaches in pastry-lined 9-inch pie plate; pour brown sugar mixture over. Adjust lattice crust; seal. Bake in hot oven (400°) about 35 minutes. Cool before serving.

## DEEP DISH ORANGE PEACH PIE

Combine ¾ cup sugar, 3 tablespoons all-purpose flour, 1 teaspoon grated orange peel, and dash nutmeg. Mix with 2 cups orange sections, cut up, and one 1-pound 13-ounce can sliced peaches, drained. Turn into 8x8x2-inch baking dish. Dot with 2 tablespoons butter or margarine.

Prepare pastry based on 1½ cups flour. Roll to ⅛ inch; cut in 9-inch square. Place atop filling, cutting slits for escape of steam. Crimp to edges of baking dish. Bake at 400° about 40 minutes. Serve warm; top with ice cream.

## PIZZA PEACH PIE

½ cup butter or margarine
¼ cup sifted confectioners' sugar
1 cup sifted all-purpose flour
2 tablespoons cornstarch
2 tablespoons granulated sugar
¼ teaspoon mace
⅔ cup orange juice
½ cup red currant jelly
1 1-pound 13-ounce can sliced peaches, well drained

*Crust:* Cream together butter or margarine and confectioners' sugar. Blend in flour to make soft dough. Pat evenly onto bottom and sides of 12-inch pizza pan; prick well with fork. Bake in moderate oven (350°) for 15 to 20 minutes.

*Filling:* Combine cornstarch, granulated sugar, and mace in small saucepan. Stir in orange juice; add jelly. Cook and stir till mixture thickens and boils; cook 2 minutes more. Cool slightly. Arrange peaches in single layer in baked shell, forming circles, one inside the other. Spoon glaze over. Chill. Trim with whipped cream. Makes 10 to 12 servings.

## GOLDEN PEACH PIE

2 1-pound cans sliced peaches
½ cup sugar
2 tablespoons all-purpose flour
¼ teaspoon nutmeg
Dash salt
2 tablespoons butter or margarine
1 tablespoon lemon juice
½ teaspoon grated orange peel
⅛ teaspoon almond extract
Pastry for 9-inch lattice-top pie

Drain peaches, reserving ⅓ cup syrup. Combine sugar, flour, nutmeg, and salt; add reserved syrup. Cook and stir till mixture thickens. Add next 4 ingredients, then peaches. Line 9-inch pie plate with pastry; fill. Adjust lattice top; seal. Sprinkle with sugar. Bake in hot oven (400°) 40 to 45 minutes. If pie browns too quickly, cover edge with foil. Serve warm.

Who could refuse a piece of sugar-crusted Golden Peach Pie warm from the oven! Subtle flavor includes almond and nutmeg.

## RED CHERRY PIE

¾ cup juice from cherries
¾ cup sugar
1½ tablespoons quick-cooking tapioca
1 1-pound 4-ounce can (2 cups) pitted
    tart red cherries (water pack),*
    well drained
Red food coloring
3 or 4 drops almond extract (optional)
Dash salt
Pastry for 8-inch lattice-top pie
1 tablespoon butter or margarine

Combine first 7 ingredients; let stand 20 minutes. Line 8-inch pie plate with pastry; fill with cherry mixture. Dot with butter. Adjust lattice top; seal. Bake at 400° for 50 to 55 minutes.

*For frozen pitted tart red cherries, thawed, decrease sugar to ⅓ cup and omit food coloring.

When fresh cherries are available, make this very special **Fresh Cherry Pie.** Prepare pastry for 8-inch lattice-top pie; line 8-inch pie plate with pastry. Combine 3 cups pitted fresh ripe tart red cherries (pit with small paper clip spread open), 1 to 1½ cups sugar, ¼ cup all-purpose flour, and dash salt. Turn into pastry-lined pie plate; dot with 2 tablespoons butter or margarine. Adjust lattice top; seal. Bake at 400° for about 50 to 55 minutes. Serve warm.

## CHERRY-CHEESE PIZZA

Pastry for 2-crust 9-inch pie
1 8-ounce package cream cheese, softened
½ cup sugar
2 eggs
1 teaspoon vanilla
⅓ cup chopped California walnuts
⅓ cup sugar
2 tablespoons cornstarch
Dash salt
1 1-pound 4-ounce can frozen pitted
    tart red cherries, thawed
1 tablespoon butter or margarine
Few drops almond extract
Few drops red food coloring

Roll pastry on lightly floured surface to 14-inch circle ⅛-inch thick. Place in 12-inch pizza pan; turn up and flute edges; prick crust. Bake in moderate oven (350°) for 15 minutes.

Blend cream cheese and ½ cup sugar; add eggs and beat well. Add vanilla and nuts. Pour into partially baked crust and continue to bake in moderate oven 10 minutes, or till done.

Meanwhile, combine ⅓ cup sugar, cornstarch, and salt. Add cherries; cook and stir over low heat till thickened. Add butter, almond extract, and food coloring. (Or use one 1-pound 5-ounce can cherry pie filling.) Spread over cheese layer. To serve, cut in wedges and trim with whipped cream. Makes 10 to 12 servings.

## DOUBLE-CRUST CHERRY PIE

1½ cups sugar
4 tablespoons cornstarch
¾ cup cherry juice
3 cups canned pitted tart red cherries
    (water pack)
1 tablespoon butter or margarine
¼ teaspoon red food coloring
Pastry for 2-crust 9-inch pie

Combine ¾ *cup* of the sugar with cornstarch. Stir in cherry juice. Cook over medium heat, stirring occasionally, till mixture thickens and boils; cook 1 minute longer. Add remaining ¾ cup sugar, cherries, butter, and food coloring. Let stand while preparing pastry. Line 9-inch pie plate with pastry; fill. Adjust top crust, cutting slits for escape of steam. Bake in hot oven (400°) for 55 minutes or till top is browned.

## CHERRY-RASPBERRY PIE

*Enjoy double-fruit flavor in our cover pie—*

Pastry for 2-crust 9-inch pie
1 10-ounce package frozen raspberries,
    thawed
1 1-pound 4-ounce can frozen pitted
    tart red cherries, thawed
¾ cup sugar
3 tablespoons cornstarch
¼ teaspoon salt
Few drops red food coloring

Drain raspberries and cherries (reserve syrup); add enough cherry syrup to raspberry syrup to make 1 cup. Blend sugar, cornstarch, and salt in saucepan; stir in syrup and food coloring. Add cherries. Cook and stir over low heat till thick. Stir in raspberries. Turn into pastry-lined 9-inch pie plate. Adjust top crust, cutting slits or cherry design for escape of steam; seal. Bake in hot oven (425°) about 35 minutes.

*Note:* Two cups pitted fresh ripe tart red cherries may be substituted for the frozen cherries. Add water to raspberry syrup to make 1 cup.

## CRUMB TOP PLUM PIE

*Pie bakers often neglect to use this delicious fruit—*

1¾ pounds fresh Italian plums,
    pitted and quartered (4½ cups)
⅓ cup water
¾ to 1 cup sugar
3 tablespoons cornstarch
¼ teaspoon salt
1 *unbaked* 9-inch pastry shell
⅓ cup sifted all-purpose flour
⅓ cup sugar
½ teaspoon cinnamon
¼ teaspoon nutmeg
3 tablespoons butter or margarine

Combine plums and water; bring to boiling and cook 3 to 4 minutes. Mix ¾ cup sugar, cornstarch, and salt; stir into plum mixture. Cook slowly, stirring constantly, till thick and clear, about 5 minutes. Remove from heat; cool. Turn into pastry shell. Combine flour, ⅓ cup sugar, cinnamon, and nutmeg. Cut in butter till crumbly. Sprinkle over top of pie. Bake in hot oven (400°) 30 to 35 minutes.

## STRAWBERRY-RHUBARB PIE

1½ cups sugar
3 tablespoons quick-cooking tapioca
¼ teaspoon salt
¼ teaspoon nutmeg
1 pound rhubarb, cut in ½-inch
    pieces (3 cups)
1 cup sliced fresh strawberries
Pastry for 9-inch lattice-top pie
1 tablespoon butter or margarine

Combine first 4 ingredients. Add rhubarb and strawberries; mix to coat fruit. Let stand about 20 minutes. Turn into pastry-lined 9-inch pie plate. Dot with butter. Adjust lattice top; seal. Bake at 400° for 35 to 40 minutes.

## STRAWBERRY GLAZE PIE

4 cups fresh strawberries
1 cup water
¾ cup sugar
3 tablespoons cornstarch
Few drops red food coloring
1 *baked* 8-inch pastry shell

Crush *1 cup* of the smaller berries and cook with water about 2 minutes; sieve. Combine sugar and cornstarch; stir into berry juice. Cook and stir till clear. Add food coloring. Place *half* the berries in pastry shell; pour *half* the sauce over. Repeat with remaining berries and sauce. Chill. Serve with whipped cream.

## STRAWBERRY GLAMOUR PIE

*In this pie, you'll find the meringue under the filling—*

Beat 2 egg whites with ½ teaspoon vinegar and ¼ teaspoon salt to soft peaks. Gradually add ⅓ cup sugar, beating to stiff peaks. Spread on bottom and sides of *baked* 9-inch pastry shell. Bake in slow oven (325°) 12 minutes; cool.

Mash ½ cup fresh strawberries with ¼ cup sugar. Combine 1 tablespoon cornstarch and ½ cup cold water; stir in mashed berries. Cook and stir till mixture boils; cook 2 minutes longer. Stir in few drops red food coloring and 1½ cups sliced fresh strawberries; cool slightly. Spread over meringue; chill. Spread with ½ cup whipping cream, whipped.

Cheddar cheese triangles melt over a crunchy spice crumb topping on Pear Crumble Pie. Serve this pie still warm and fragrant from the oven and win your family's praise.

## PEAR CRUMBLE PIE

6 medium Bartlett pears, pared
3 tablespoons lemon juice
½ cup sugar
2 tablespoons all-purpose flour
1 teaspoon grated lemon peel
1 *unbaked* 9-inch pastry shell
Crumble Topping
3 slices sharp process American cheese

Slice 5 pears; cut remaining pear in sixths. Sprinkle pears with lemon juice. Mix sugar, flour, and lemon peel; stir into sliced pears. Spoon into pastry shell. Arrange pear wedges atop sliced pears. Sprinkle with Crumble Topping. Bake at 400° for 45 minutes or till pears are tender. Remove from oven. Cut cheese slices in half diagonally and arrange on pie. Serve warm. *Crumble Topping:* Mix ½ cup all-purpose flour, ½ cup sugar, ½ teaspoon *each* ginger and cinnamon, and ¼ teaspoon mace. Cut in 4 tablespoons butter or margarine till crumbly.

## BLUEBERRY PIE

Prepare pastry for 2-crust 9-inch pie and line pie plate with pastry. Combine 4 cups fresh blueberries with ¾ to 1 cup sugar, 3 tablespoons all-purpose flour, ½ teaspoon grated lemon peel, dash salt, and if desired, ½ teaspoon *each* cinnamon and nutmeg. Fill pie shell. Drizzle with 1 to 2 teaspoons lemon juice; dot with 1 tablespoon butter. Cut slits; adjust top crust; seal. Bake at 400° for 35 to 40 minutes.

## ROSY RASPBERRY PIE

Partially defrost two 10-ounce packages frozen red raspberries. Combine 3 tablespoons quick-cooking tapioca, ⅔ cup sugar, and dash salt; mix with fruit and let stand 15 minutes. Meanwhile, make pastry for 9-inch lattice-top pie and line pie plate with pastry. Spoon berry mixture into shell; adjust lattice top; seal. Bake in hot oven (425°) 35 to 40 minutes.

# PEAR-APPLE CRUMB PIE

1 1-pound 13-ounce can (3½ cups) pear
    halves, drained
2 to 3 tart apples, pared, cored, and
    sliced (2 cups)
⅓ cup sugar
2 tablespoons all-purpose flour
½ teaspoon cinnamon
¼ teaspoon salt
½ cup raisins
½ teaspoon grated lemon peel
1 tablespoon lemon juice
1 *unbaked* 9-inch pastry shell
Crumb Topping

Slice pear halves and add sliced apples. Combine sugar, flour, cinnamon, and salt. Add to fruit along with raisins, lemon peel, and lemon juice. Turn into pastry shell. Sprinkle with Crumb Topping. Bake in hot oven (400°) for 15 minutes. Cover with foil and bake for 20 to 30 minutes more, or till apples are tender.

*Crumb Topping:* Combine ½ cup brown sugar, ¼ cup all-purpose flour, and ½ teaspoon salt. Cut in 4 tablespoons butter till crumbly; stir in ½ cup chopped California walnuts.

# ISLAND PIE

*Easiest pie you will ever make—just 4 ingredients—*

Swirl ½ cup dairy sour cream in one 1-pound 6-ounce can apricot pie filling till almost blended. Turn into 9-inch graham-cracker crust. Sprinkle 1 cup flaked coconut, toasted, over filling. Chill thoroughly, about 4 hours.

# CONCORD GRAPE PIE

Slip skins from 1½ pounds (4 cups) Concord grapes; set skins aside. Bring pulp to boil; reduce heat and simmer 5 minutes. Press through sieve to remove seeds. Add skins to pulp.

Combine 1 cup sugar, ⅓ cup all-purpose flour, and ¼ teaspoon salt. Add 1 tablespoon lemon juice, 2 tablespoons butter or margarine, melted, and grape mixture. Pour into *unbaked* 9-inch pastry shell. Sift ½ cup all-purpose flour with ½ cup sugar. Cut in ¼ cup butter or margarine till crumbly. Sprinkle over pie. Bake in hot oven (400°) about 40 minutes.

# FRESH GOOSEBERRY PIE

Prepare pastry for 2-crust 9-inch pie and line pie plate with pastry. Crush ½ cup gooseberries; combine with 1½ cups sugar, 3 tablespoons quick-cooking tapioca, and ¼ teaspoon salt. Cook and stir till mixture thickens and boils. Add 2½ cups whole berries. Fill pastry shell. Dot with 2 tablespoons butter or margarine. Adjust top crust, cutting slits for escape of steam; seal. Bake in a hot oven (400°) 30 to 40 minutes or till crust is browned. Serve warm.

# FRESH APRICOT PIE

*Fresh flavor and golden color make this pie a winner—*

Prepare pastry for 2-crust 9-inch pie and line pie plate with pastry; fill with 3 cups fresh apricot halves. Combine 1 cup sugar, 3 tablespoons all-purpose flour, and ¼ teaspoon nutmeg; sprinkle over apricots. Drizzle 1 tablespoon lemon juice over fruit and dot with 1 tablespoon butter or margarine. Adjust top crust, cutting slits for escape of steam; seal. Bake in hot oven (425°) about 25 to 30 minutes.

# PEAR PINEAPPLE CHEESE PIE

1 1-pound can sliced pears
1 1-pound 4½-ounce can pineapple
    tidbits
¼ cup sugar
3 tablespoons quick-cooking tapioca
4 ounces sharp process American
    cheese, shredded (1 cup)
¼ teaspoon vanilla
Dash ginger
1 *unbaked* 9-inch pastry shell
½ cup dairy sour cream
1 tablespoon confectioners' sugar

Drain sliced pears, reserving ½ cup syrup; cut into 1-inch pieces. Drain pineapple, reserving ½ cup syrup. Combine reserved syrups, sugar, and tapioca in saucepan. Cook and stir over medium heat till mixture thickens and boils. Remove from heat and stir in cheese, vanilla, and ginger. Add pears and pineapple; turn into pastry shell. Bake in hot oven (400°) 35 to 40 minutes. Cool. Combine sour cream and sugar; spoon dollops atop pie before serving.

A star-shaped cutout adds a festive touch to spicy Mock Mince Pie. Jellied cranberry sauce sparks the spicy flavor of this pie.

## MOCK MINCE PIE

Pastry for 2-crust 9-inch pie
1⅓ cups sugar
½ teaspoon salt
½ teaspoon cinnamon
¼ teaspoon cloves
¼ teaspoon ginger
1 cup raisins
⅓ cup chopped California walnuts
1 teaspoon grated orange peel
½ teaspoon grated lemon peel
¼ cup lemon juice
½ cup canned jellied cranberry sauce,
   crushed
1½ cups finely chopped apple

Mix sugar, salt, and spices. Add remaining ingredients; mix well. Turn into pastry-lined 9-inch pie plate. With cookie cutter or knife, cut out star in center of top crust; adjust top crust over filling; seal. Sprinkle with red decorating sugar. Bake in hot oven (400°) about 30 to 35 minutes or till browned. Serve warm.

## MINCEMEAT PIE

Pastry for 2-crust 8-inch pie
1 9-ounce package mincemeat
   (dry)
1 8½-ounce can (1 cup) applesauce
¼ cup sugar
1½ cups water
2 tablespoons dry sherry wine

Break up mincemeat and combine with applesauce, sugar, and water in a saucepan. Stir over heat till lumps are completely broken. Boil about 1 minute, stirring constantly. Cool. Stir in wine and mix well. Turn into pastry-lined 8-inch pie plate. Adjust top crust, cutting slits for escape of steam; seal. Bake in a hot oven (425°) about 30 to 35 minutes or till browned.

## PINEAPPLE-APRICOT PIE

Pastry for 9-inch lattice-top pie
¾ cup sugar
1 tablespoon all-purpose flour
2 cups dried apricots, cooked
1 8¾-ounce can crushed pineapple,
   drained
1 tablespoon butter or margarine

Combine sugar and flour; sprinkle *1 tablespoon* mixture in pastry-lined 9-inch pie plate. Add remaining mixture to cooked apricots and pineapple. Toss till fruit is coated. Turn into pastry; dot with butter. Adjust lattice top; seal. Bake in hot oven (425°) for 40 to 45 minutes.

## PINEAPPLE-RHUBARB PIE

*Surprise! Looks like rhubarb, tastes like pineapple—*

Pastry for 9-inch lattice-top pie
3 cups fresh rhubarb cut in ½-inch
   pieces (about 1 pound)
1 8¾-ounce can crushed pineapple,
   *undrained*
1¼ cups sugar
⅓ cup sifted all-purpose flour
2 tablespoons butter or margarine

Mix rhubarb and pineapple. Combine sugar, flour, and dash salt; toss with fruits. Turn into pastry-lined pie plate. Dot with butter. Adjust lattice top; seal. Bake at 400° for 40 minutes.

# FRUIT CUP PIE

Pastry for 2-crust 9-inch pie

. . .

¾ cup sugar
2½ tablespoons quick-cooking tapioca
¼ teaspoon cinnamon
¼ teaspoon nutmeg
Dash salt
2 cups diced peaches
2 cups diced pears
1 cup seedless green grapes
1 tablespoon chopped maraschino cherries
1 tablespoon lemon juice
1 tablespoon butter or margarine

Mix sugar, tapioca, spices, and salt. Add fruits and lemon juice; mix lightly. Turn into pastry-lined 9-inch pie plate. Dot with butter. Adjust top crust, cutting slits for escape of steam; seal. Brush crust with milk; sprinkle lightly with sugar. Bake in hot oven (400°) about 30 minutes. Serve slightly warm.

# RHUBARB PIE

Prepare pastry for 2-crust 9-inch pie. Combine 4 cups fresh rhubarb cut in 1-inch pieces (about 1 pound), 1⅔ cups sugar, ⅓ cup sifted all-purpose flour, and dash salt. Let stand 15 minutes. Turn into pastry-lined 9-inch pie plate. Dot with 2 tablespoons butter or margarine. Adjust top crust, cutting slits for escape of steam; seal. Bake at 400° for 50 minutes.

# FRESH PINEAPPLE PIE

Prepare pastry for 2-crust 9-inch pie. Mix ¾ cup sugar, 3 tablespoons quick-cooking tapioca, and dash salt; add to 4 cups fresh pineapple chunks with 1 teaspoon grated lemon peel and 1 tablespoon lemon juice. Let stand 15 minutes. Turn into pastry-lined 9-inch pie plate. Dot with 1 tablespoon butter. Adjust top crust, cutting slits for escape of steam; seal. Bake at 425° about 45 minutes or till lightly browned.

Three fresh fruits combine to make a colorful pie that is bound to be a favorite with your family. Fruit Cup Pie served warm with ice cream is a real hearty treat.

Serve little pies, such as Petite Peach Pies, for a big occasion. With apricot-sherry glaze, they taste like the specialty of a fine French restaurant. Serve with cups of steaming coffee.

# PETITE FRUIT PIES

## PETITE PEACH PIES

1 *teaspoon* unflavored gelatin
2 tablespoons cold water
1 12-ounce jar (1 cup) apricot preserves
¼ cup cream sherry
Dash salt
4 *ripe* peaches, peeled and halved, *or*
    1 1-pound 13-ounce can peach halves, well drained
8 *baked* 3½-inch pastry shells
½ cup whipping cream, whipped

Soften gelatin in cold water. Heat preserves to boiling; add gelatin; stir to dissolve. Add sherry and salt. Cool till slightly thickened. Place peach half, cut side down, in tart shell. Spoon preserve mixture over. Chill. Serve with whipped cream and a stemmed maraschino cherry.

## CRAN-APPLE TARTS

1 cup cranberries, cut in half
½ cup sugar
1 stick pie crust mix
1 1-pound 4-ounce can (2½ cups) apple pie filling
½ teaspoon vanilla
2 tablespoons butter or margarine

Mix cranberries and sugar; let stand 1 hour. Prepare pie crust mix according to package directions; roll to ⅛ inch. Cut in 6 circles, 1 inch larger in diameter than 6-ounce custard cups. Combine pie filling and vanilla; stir in cranberries. Divide into 6 custard cups. Dot with butter. Top with pastry; crimp edges of pastry to edges of baking cups. Cut slits in tops. Bake in a hot oven (425°) for 25 minutes or till done.

## STRAWBERRY-CHEESE TARTS

Prepare graham-cracker crust (see index). Press into eight 3½-inch tart pans; chill. Sprinkle ¼ cup sugar over 2 cups sliced fresh strawberries; let stand. Drain, reserving ¼ cup syrup. Soften 1½ *teaspoons* unflavored gelatin in reserved syrup; dissolve over hot water.

Beat one 3-ounce package cream cheese with ¼ cup sugar till fluffy; add dissolved gelatin. Have one 6-ounce can (⅔ cup) evaporated milk *chilled icy-cold*. In chilled bowl, whip milk till fluffy; add 2 tablespoons lemon juice and beat to stiff peaks. Fold in cheese mixture; then fold in strawberries. Spoon into chilled tart shells. Chill till firm, about 2 hours.

## CHERRY TARTS

Drain one 1-pound 4-ounce can (2½ cups) pitted tart red cherries (water pack); add water to cherry juice to make 1 cup. Combine ½ cup sugar and 2 tablespoons cornstarch. Slowly add cherry liquid; mix well. Cook over medium heat, stirring often, till thick. Add 3 drops almond extract and 6 drops red food coloring. Cool to lukewarm. Fold in cherries. Spoon into 4 baked 3½-inch tart shells. Chill.

## CINNAMON FRUIT TARTS

8 slices white bread
¼ cup butter or margarine, melted
¼ cup sugar
1 teaspoon cinnamon
1 3¾- or 3⅝-ounce package *instant* vanilla pudding mix
¼ teaspoon rum flavoring
1 1-pound 1-ounce can fruit cocktail, drained
8 California walnut halves

Roll each slice of bread to ⅛-inch thickness; trim crust. Brush both sides with melted butter. Combine sugar and cinnamon and sprinkle one side of bread with mixture. Press into muffin cups to form shell so that plain buttered side is against muffin cup. Bake in moderate oven (375°) about 15 minutes. Prepare pudding mix according to package directions, adding rum flavoring. Spoon into shells; top with well-drained fruit cocktail and a walnut half.

Use pastry based on 2 cups flour for 6 to 8 tart shells (see index). Roll dough ⅛ inch thick. Cut in 5- or 6-inch circles. Fit over inverted muffin cups (above), or custard cups, and pinch a pleat in several places. Prick well. Bake at 450° for 10 to 12 minutes. Cool before filling.

Or fit pastry in tart pans (below). Trim pastry ½ inch beyond edge; turn under and flute. Prick bottom and sides well. Bake at 450° for 10 to 12 minutes.

Or make throw-away tart pans from aluminum foil. Roll out pastry on heavy-duty aluminum foil and cut through foil and pastry in 5-inch circles. Prick pastry well. Holding foil and pastry together (foil on outside), flute in about 5 crimps to form shells. Place on baking sheet; bake at 450° for about 10 minutes. Cool; remove foil.

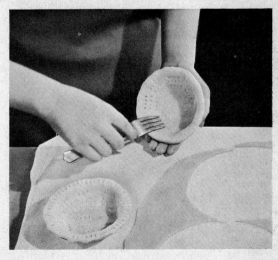

# SMOOTH CREAM PIES

## VANILLA CREAM PIE

*A basic cream pie recipe. Try the four variations, too—*

In saucepan, combine ¾ cup sugar, ⅓ cup all-purpose flour *or* 3 tablespoons cornstarch, and ¼ teaspoon salt. Gradually add 2 cups milk, mixing well. Cook and stir over medium heat till mixture thickens and boils. Cook 2 minutes longer. Remove from heat. Stir small amount hot mixture into 3 slightly beaten egg yolks; immediately return to hot mixture; cook 2 minutes, stirring constantly. Remove from heat. Add 2 tablespoons butter and 1 teaspoon vanilla. Pour into cooled *baked* 9-inch pastry shell. Spread 1 recipe Meringue (3 egg whites) atop pie and bake at 350° for 12 to 15 minutes. Cool.

Or, omit meringue and serve with whipped cream. (To prevent skin from forming on surface of filling in crust, put waxed paper directly on top, touching entire surface of hot pudding.)

## CHOCOLATE CREAM PIE

Prepare Vanilla Cream Pie, increasing sugar to 1 cup. Chop two 1-ounce squares unsweetened chocolate; add with milk. Top with Meringue (3 egg whites) and bake as directed.

## BANANA CREAM PIE

Slice 3 bananas into cooled *baked* 9-inch pastry shell; top with Vanilla Cream Pie filling and Meringue (3 egg whites). Bake as directed.

## BUTTERSCOTCH PIE

Substitute brown sugar for granulated sugar in Vanilla Cream Pie filling. Increase butter to 3 tablespoons. Top with Meringue (3 egg whites) and bake as directed.

## MERINGUE

Beat 3 egg whites with ½ teaspoon vanilla and ¼ teaspoon cream of tartar till soft peaks form. Gradually add 6 tablespoons sugar, beating till stiff peaks form and all sugar is dissolved. Spread atop pie, *sealing* to edge of pastry. Bake in moderate oven (350°) 12 to 15 minutes, or till meringue is golden. Cool.

For a smaller meringue or for a filling using only 2 egg yolks, beat *2 egg whites* with ½ teaspoon vanilla and ¼ teaspoon cream of tartar till soft peaks form. Gradually add *4 tablespoons sugar*, beating till stiff peaks form.

For a luscious **Coconut Cream Pie,** add 1 cup flaked coconut to Vanilla Cream Pie filling. Top with Meringue (3 egg whites); sprinkle with ⅓ cup coconut. Bake as directed.

Add small amount of hot mixture to beaten egg yolks; blend, return to hot mixture.

Pour hot filling into cooled, baked pastry shell. Spread meringue on the hot filling.

To prevent shrinking, carefully seal meringue to edge of pastry all the way around.

## CHERRY CHOCOLATE PIE

1 4-ounce jar maraschino cherries
1 4-ounce package *regular* chocolate
pudding mix
1 *baked* 9-inch pastry shell
1 2-ounce package dessert topping mix
¼ cup chopped pecans

Drain maraschino cherries; reserve juice and chop cherries (should have about ¼ cup juice and ⅓ cup chopped cherries). Prepare pudding mix according to package directions using cherry juice and milk to make amount of liquid called for. Cool; pour into cooled pastry shell. Chill.
   Prepare dessert topping mix according to package directions; fold in the pecans and chopped cherries. Spread over pie filling.

## CREAMY PUMPKIN WHIP PIE

Whip one 3¾-ounce package vanilla whipped dessert mix with ½ cup cold milk. Add 1 cup canned pumpkin and 1½ teaspoons pumpkin pie spice; beat. Prepare one 2-ounce package dessert topping mix with ½ cup cold milk and ½ teaspoon vanilla. Fold into pumpkin mixture. Pour into 9-inch graham-cracker crust. Chill.

## PEANUT-BUTTER PIE

⅔ cup sugar
2½ tablespoons cornstarch
1 tablespoon all-purpose flour
½ teaspoon salt
3 cups milk
3 slightly beaten egg yolks
¼ cup crunchy peanut butter
1 tablespoon butter or margarine
1 *baked* 9-inch pastry shell
1 recipe Meringue (3 egg whites)

In saucepan, combine sugar, cornstarch, flour, and salt. Add milk and cook over low heat, stirring constantly till mixture thickens and boils. Cook 2 minutes longer. Remove from heat and stir a small amount of the hot mixture into egg yolks; return to hot mixture. Cook 1 minute longer, stirring constantly. Add peanut butter and butter; stir till blended. Pour into cooled baked pastry shell. Top with meringue and bake at 350° for 12 to 15 minutes.

## LEMON MERINGUE PIE

1½ cups sugar
3 tablespoons cornstarch
3 tablespoons all-purpose flour
Dash salt
1½ cups hot water
3 slightly beaten egg yolks
2 tablespoons butter or margarine
½ teaspoon grated lemon peel
⅛ cup lemon juice
1 *baked* 9-inch pastry shell
1 recipe Meringue (3 egg whites)

In saucepan, mix first 4 ingredients; gradually add hot water, stirring constantly. Cook and stir over high heat till mixture comes to boiling. Reduce heat; cook and stir 2 minutes. Stir small amount hot mixture into egg yolks, then return to hot mixture. Bring to boiling and cook 2 minutes, stirring constantly. Add butter and lemon peel. Slowly add lemon juice, mixing well. Pour into pastry shell. Spread meringue over filling. Bake in moderate oven (350°) 12 to 15 minutes. Cool before serving.
   *Note:* For creamier filling, cook and stir first 5 ingredients 8 minutes over low heat after mixture comes to boil. Blend in egg yolks as above; cook 4 minutes after mixture boils.

## VANILLA RAISIN PIE

Simmer 1½ cups raisins in ½ cup water in covered saucepan 10 minutes. Stir in ½ teaspoon cinnamon, ½ teaspoon instant coffee powder, and dash cloves; cool. Beat one 3¾- or 3⅝-ounce package *instant* vanilla pudding mix with 1½ cups milk for 30 seconds. Stir in raisin mixture. Pour into *baked* 9-inch pastry shell. Sprinkle with ½ cup chopped walnuts. Chill.

## RUM EGGNOG PIE

Combine in a bowl one 3¾- or 3⅝-ounce package *instant* vanilla pudding mix, 1¾ cups dairy eggnog, and 1 tablespoon rum; beat for 1 minute. Pour into cooled *baked* 9-inch pastry shell; chill till filling is set. Prepare one 2-ounce package dessert topping mix according to package directions. Beat in 1 teaspoon rum. Pile over pudding in pastry shell. Chill. Top with chopped candied fruit and toasted almonds.

Perfect Lemon Meringue Pie, a real recipe classic! Not too tart, yet not too sweet, with a delicate texture that is creamy smooth, but is firm enough to hold its shape when cut.

Some lemon pies are too stiff, others run when cut, but not this one! After filling is cooked, butter and lemon peel are mixed in; then lemon juice is slowly added while stirring constantly. Lemon juice added after cooking helps prevent a runny filling.

Pour hot filling into a cooled baked pastry shell. (Note the thickness of the filling.) No need to cool the filling before topping with meringue. Carefully seal meringue to crust all around—no shrinking this way. Bake till peaks are golden brown; cool before serving.

## PINEAPPLE SOUR CREAM PIE

¾ cup sugar
¼ cup all-purpose flour
½ teaspoon salt
1 1-pound 4½-ounce can (2½ cups)
  crushed pineapple, undrained
1 cup dairy sour cream
1 tablespoon lemon juice
2 slightly beaten egg yolks
1 *baked* 9-inch pastry shell
1 recipe Meringue (2 egg whites)

In saucepan, combine sugar, flour, and salt. Stir in next 3 ingredients. Cook and stir till mixture thickens and comes to boiling; cook 2 minutes. Stir small amount of hot mixture into egg yolks; return to hot mixture, stirring constantly. Cook and stir 2 minutes. Spoon into cooled pastry shell. Spread meringue atop pie, sealing meringue to crust, and bake in a moderate oven (350°) for 12 to 15 minutes.

## SPICED BUTTERSCOTCH PIE

1 stick pie crust mix
3 tablespoons finely chopped walnuts
1 4-ounce package *regular* butterscotch
  pudding mix
½ teaspoon cinnamon
¼ teaspoon nutmeg
Dash ginger
½ cup whipping cream, whipped
Broken California walnuts

Prepare and roll out 1 stick pastry mix according to package directions; sprinkle with finely chopped nuts and roll in lightly. Fit pastry into an 8-inch pie plate; flute edge. Prick the bottom and sides well with fork. Bake, following package directions; cool.

Prepare pudding mix according to package directions, adding spices to dry mix. Cool 5 minutes; turn into cooled pastry shell. Chill. Top with whipped cream; sprinkle with walnuts.

Pineapple Sour Cream Pie has sunny tropical flavor with the extra tang of dairy sour cream. A puff of airy meringue baked to golden perfection covers the creamy pineapple filling. A deliciously different flavor combination.

## COCOA-CRUST LIME PIE

1 cup sifted all-purpose flour
¼ cup instant cocoa (dry)
½ teaspoon salt
⅓ cup shortening
3 tablespoons milk
½ teaspoon vanilla
1¼ cups sugar
½ cup sifted all-purpose flour
¼ teaspoon salt
½ cup frozen limeade concentrate, thawed
1 drop green food coloring
3 slightly beaten egg yolks
3 tablespoons butter or margarine
½ cup whipping cream, whipped

To make crust, sift together 1 cup flour, cocoa, and ½ teaspoon salt; cut in shortening. Combine milk and vanilla; stir into dry ingredients till mixture is moistened and forms a ball. Roll out between waxed paper (do not add extra flour). Line 9-inch pie plate; flute edge. Prick bottom and sides. Bake at 400° for 10 minutes.

*Filling:* In saucepan, mix sugar, ½ cup flour, and ¼ teaspoon salt. Slowly stir in 1¾ cups water. Add limeade and food coloring. Cook and stir till mixture thickens and boils; cook 2 minutes. Stir a small amount of hot mixture into egg yolks; return to hot mixture. Stir and cook till mixture boils; add butter. Pour into crust. Cool; top with whipping cream. Chill 3 to 4 hours or till ready to serve.

## CHOCOLATE PEANUT PIE

1 4-ounce package *regular* chocolate pudding mix
¼ cup peanut butter
1 2-ounce package dessert topping mix
1 *baked* 9-inch pastry shell
2 tablespoons peanuts, chopped

Prepare pudding mix according to package directions, using 1¾ *cups milk*. Add small amount of hot pudding to peanut butter; beat till smooth; beat into remaining pudding. Cover surface and cool, stirring once or twice. Prepare dessert topping mix according to package directions; reserve ½ cup. Fold remaining topping into pudding. Pile into pastry shell; chill. Top with reserved dessert topping and nuts.

## CHERRY CREAM PIE

1 8-ounce package cream cheese, softened
1 cup dairy sour cream
½ cup milk
1 3¾- or 3⅝-ounce package *instant* vanilla pudding mix
1 1-pound 5-ounce can cherry pie filling
1 *baked* 9-inch pastry shell

Beat together first 3 ingredients using slow speed on mixer. Fold in pudding mix. Reserve ½ cup cherry filling; marble remainder into pudding mixture. Pour into pie shell; top with remaining cherry filling; chill thoroughly.

## LEMON RAISIN PIE

Pastry for 2-crust 9-inch pie
2 cups raisins
1 3⅝-ounce package *regular* lemon pudding and pie filling mix
1 tablespoon butter or margarine

Pour boiling water over raisins and let stand 10 minutes; drain. Prepare lemon pudding mix according to package directions. Stir in butter or margarine and raisins. Line pie plate with pastry; fill with raisin mixture. Adjust top crust, cutting slits for escape of steam; seal and crimp edge. Bake in hot oven (400°) 35 to 40 minutes, or till crust is lightly browned.

## PINEAPPLE TAPIOCA PIE

1 3-ounce package lemon-flavored gelatin
1 3¼-ounce package vanilla tapioca pudding mix
1¾ cups milk
1 8¾-ounce can crushed pineapple
1 2-ounce package dessert topping mix
1 *baked* 9-inch pastry shell

In a saucepan, combine gelatin and pudding mix. Stir in milk. Over medium heat, bring to full boil (mixture may look separated before it comes to boil). Chill till partially set. Fold in *undrained* pineapple. Prepare dessert topping mix according to package directions. Fold half into pudding mixture, reserving remaining for garnish. Turn into pastry shell. Chill till firm. Garnish with remaining dessert topping.

Glazed strawberry petal top makes a real beauty of a pie. Strawberry Pineapple Cream Pie has a creamy layer made easy with vanilla pudding mix and canned pineapple.

## STRAWBERRY PINEAPPLE CREAM PIE

Prepare one 3- or 3¼-ounce package *regular* vanilla pudding mix according to package directions *using 1½ cups milk*. Cool slightly without stirring. Fold in one 8¾-ounce can crushed pineapple, *well drained* (⅔ cup). Fold in 1 teaspoon vanilla and ½ cup whipping cream, whipped. Spread in cooled *baked* 9-inch pastry shell. Chill till set.

In small saucepan, crush ½ cup fresh strawberries; add ½ cup water. Cook 2 minutes and sieve. Combine ¼ cup sugar and 2 teaspoons cornstarch; gradually stir in sieved berries. Return mixture to saucepan and cook, stirring constantly, till thick and clear. Tint to desired color with red food coloring.

Slice 2½ cups strawberries in half lengthwise, reserving a few perfect whole berries for center of pie. Arrange berries over cream filling; spoon strawberry glaze over. Chill several hours. Serve topped with whipped cream.

## SPEEDY CHEESECAKE PIE

1 8-ounce package cream cheese, softened
½ cup sugar
1 tablespoon lemon juice
½ teaspoon vanilla
Dash salt
2 eggs
1 *unbaked* 8-inch graham-cracker crust
1 cup dairy sour cream
2 tablespoons sugar
½ teaspoon vanilla

Beat cream cheese till fluffy; gradually blend in ½ cup sugar, lemon juice, ½ teaspoon vanilla, and salt. Add eggs, one at a time, beating well after each. Pour filling into crust. Bake in slow oven (325°) 25 to 30 minutes or till set. Combine remaining ingredients and spoon over top of pie. Bake 10 minutes longer. Cool. Chill several hours. Serve with fresh ripe strawberries or other fresh or frozen fruit, if desired.

# CUSTARD-TYPE PIES

## CUSTARD PIE

Blend 4 slightly beaten eggs, $\frac{1}{2}$ cup sugar, $\frac{1}{4}$ teaspoon salt, and $\frac{1}{2}$ teaspoon vanilla. Gradually stir in $2\frac{1}{2}$ cups milk, scalded; pour into *unbaked* 9-inch pastry shell. Sprinkle with nutmeg. Bake in moderate oven (350°) 35 to 40 minutes or till knife inserted halfway between center and edge comes out clean. Cool on rack.

*Note:* If desired, omit nutmeg and sprinkle top of unbaked filling with $\frac{1}{2}$ cup flaked coconut.

## SLIPPED CUSTARD PIE

*Flaky pastry contrasts with smooth custard—*

Prepare filling for Custard Pie. Place buttered 8-inch pie plate in shallow baking pan. Fill pie plate with custard (pour extra into custard cups and bake with pie filling). Fill baking pan with cold water. Bake in a moderate oven (350°) for 35 to 40 minutes or till knife comes out clean. Remove pie to cooling rack. When filling is cool, carefully run spatula around edge. Shake plate gently to loosen custard. Hold custard just above far rim of baked 9-inch pastry shell; gently slip into shell. Chill.

## COCONUT TARTS

*Tart shells:* Prepare pastry based on 2 cups flour. Roll $\frac{1}{8}$ inch thick; cut in eight 5- or 6-inch circles. Line 8 muffin pans or eight $3\frac{1}{4}$x $1\frac{1}{4}$-inch fluted tart pans with pastry.

*Filling:* Combine 3 beaten eggs, $1\frac{1}{2}$ cups sugar, $\frac{1}{2}$ cup butter or margarine, melted, 4 teaspoons lemon juice, and 1 teaspoon vanilla; stir in one $3\frac{1}{2}$-ounce can ($1\frac{1}{3}$ cups) flaked coconut. Pour into *unbaked* tart shells. Bake in moderate oven (350°) 40 minutes or till knife inserted off center comes out clean. Cool.

## APRICOT-BUTTERMILK PIE

*For buttermilk fans—a delicate custard atop apricots—*

Simmer 1 cup dried apricot halves with $\frac{1}{4}$ cup sugar and $1\frac{1}{2}$ cups water about 25 minutes.

Blend together 2 beaten eggs, 2 cups buttermilk, $\frac{3}{4}$ cup sugar, and dash salt. Spread apricot mixture evenly in bottom of *unbaked* 9-inch pastry shell (have edges crimped high). Slowly pour buttermilk filling over apricots. Bake in a hot oven (400°) for 40 to 45 minutes or till knife comes out clean. Cool.

To prevent spills, place pastry shell on oven rack, then fill with custard mixture.

Custard pie is done when knife inserted halfway between center and edge comes out clean.

## TWO-TONE HOLIDAY PIE

*Two holiday favorites baked in one pie—*

- 1½ cups canned mincemeat
- 1 *unbaked* 9-inch pastry shell
- 1 1-pound 2-ounce can pumpkin pie filling
- ¼ cup orange juice
- 1 cup evaporated milk
- ½ teaspoon grated orange peel
- Whipped cream or dessert topping

Spread mincemeat evenly in bottom of pastry shell. Prepare pumpkin pie filling, following label directions, but *substitute the orange juice and evaporated milk for the liquid called for;* stir in peel. Pour over mincemeat in shell.

Bake in a hot oven (400°) for about 45 minutes or till knife inserted halfway between center and edge of filling comes out clean. Cool. Serve garnished with rosettes of whipped cream or whipped dessert topping.

## GRANDMA'S PUMPKIN PIE

*Taste the filling before you add all the spice, then you can have it just as you like best—*

- 1½ cups canned pumpkin
- ¾ cup sugar
- ½ teaspoon salt
- 1 to 1¼ teaspoons cinnamon
- ½ to 1 teaspoon ginger
- ¼ to ½ teaspoon nutmeg
- ¼ to ½ teaspoon cloves
- 3 slightly beaten eggs
- 1¼ cups milk
- 1 6-ounce can (⅔ cup) evaporated milk
- 1 *unbaked* 9-inch pastry shell

Combine first 7 ingredients. Blend in eggs, milk, and evaporated milk. Pour into pastry shell (have edges crimped high because amount of filling is generous). Bake in hot oven (400°) 50 minutes, or till knife inserted halfway between center and edge comes out clean. Cool.

Two-tone Holiday Pie is a grand finale for a festive meal. Velvety pumpkin custard and rich mincemeat, traditional favorites, get a speedy start from convenience foods.

## PUMPKIN ORANGE CRUNCH PIE

*Pumpkin custard boasts a crunchy, baked-on topping—*

1 cup brown sugar
1 tablespoon cornstarch
1½ teaspoons pumpkin pie spice
¼ teaspoon salt
1 1-pound can (2 cups) pumpkin
1 14½-ounce can (1⅔ cups) evaporated milk
2 slightly beaten eggs
1 *unbaked* 9-inch pastry shell
. . .
1 tablespoon brown sugar
1 tablespoon butter or margarine
1 tablespoon all-purpose flour
½ cup chopped California walnuts
2 teaspoons grated orange peel

Combine 1 cup brown sugar, cornstarch, pie spice, salt, and pumpkin. Stir in milk and eggs. Pour into pastry shell. (Crimp edges high—filling is generous.) Bake at 400° for 40 minutes. Meanwhile, combine remaining ingredients. Spoon over pie; return to oven and bake 5 to 10 minutes more or till knife comes out clean. Cool.

## CHESS PIE

½ cup butter or margarine
2 cups sugar
1 tablespoon all-purpose flour
1 tablespoon yellow cornmeal
5 well beaten eggs
1 cup milk
1 teaspoon vanilla
2 tablespoons lemon juice
1 *unbaked* Rich Pastry Shell

Cream butter and sugar; add flour and cornmeal. Add eggs, milk, vanilla, and lemon juice; beat well. Pour into pastry shell. Bake in moderate oven (350°) 55 to 60 minutes, or till knife comes out clean.

*Rich Pastry Shell:* Sift together 1 cup sifted all-purpose flour, ¼ teaspoon salt, and ¼ teaspoon baking powder. Cut in 6 tablespoons butter or margarine till the size of small peas. Add 3 to 4 tablespoons milk gradually, mixing till dough can be formed into a ball. Roll out and fit into 9-inch pie plate (have edges crimped high because amount of filling is generous).

## PECAN PIE

Cream ¼ cup butter or margarine and ½ cup sugar till fluffy. Add 1 cup dark corn syrup and ¼ teaspoon salt; beat well. Add 3 eggs one at a time beating well after each addition. Stir in 1 cup pecan halves. Pour into *unbaked* 9-inch pastry shell. Bake at 350° for 45 to 50 minutes or till knife comes out clean. Cool.

## SHOOFLY PIE

Sift together 1½ cups sifted all-purpose flour, ½ cup sugar, and ¼ teaspoon soda. Cut in ¼ cup butter or margarine till crumbly. Combine ½ cup light molasses, ¼ teaspoon soda, and ½ cup hot water. Pour ⅓ liquid in *unbaked* 8-inch pastry shell; sprinkle with ⅓ flour mixture. Repeat layers, ending with flour mixture. Bake in a moderate oven (375°) about 40 minutes. Cool.

## SOUTHERN-STYLE RAISIN PIE

Gradually add 1 cup sugar to 2 beaten eggs. Add 6 tablespoons melted butter or margarine and ¼ cup milk. Stir in 1 cup raisins and ½ cup broken pecans. Pour into *unbaked* 8-inch pastry shell. Bake in moderate oven (350°) 40 to 45 minutes. Cool. Serve with whipped cream.

## MACADAMIA NUT PIE

¼ cup sifted all-purpose flour
2 tablespoons sugar
¼ teaspoon salt
1 cup light corn syrup
1 cup honey
4 slightly beaten eggs
½ teaspoon vanilla
3 tablespoons butter or margarine, melted
1 *unbaked* 9-inch pastry shell
¾ cup coarsely broken macadamia nuts
½ cup whipping cream, whipped

Blend flour, sugar, and salt; add corn syrup and honey. Combine eggs, vanilla, and melted butter; stir into syrup mixture. Pour into pastry shell. Sprinkle with nuts. Bake in moderate oven (350°) 55 to 60 minutes or till knife inserted halfway between center and edge comes out clean. Cool. Top with whipped cream if desired.

# FLUFFY CHIFFON PIES

## ORANGE CHIFFON PIE

1 envelope (1 tablespoon) unflavored
  gelatin
1 cup sugar
¼ teaspoon salt
¾ cup milk
3 slightly beaten egg yolks

    • • •

1 teaspoon grated orange peel
¾ cup orange juice
½ teaspoon grated lemon peel
¼ cup lemon juice
1 cup whipping cream, whipped
1 *baked* 9-inch pastry shell

Combine gelatin, sugar, and salt in saucepan. Add milk and egg yolks. Cook and stir over medium heat till mixture thickens slightly. Remove from heat; add juices and peels. Chill till partially set. Fold in whipped cream. Chill till mixture mounds. Pile into pastry shell. Chill.

## MAPLE CHIFFON PIE

1 envelope (1 tablespoon)
  unflavored gelatin
¼ cup cold water
1 cup maple-flavored syrup
3 slightly beaten egg yolks
½ teaspoon salt
½ teaspoon vanilla
3 stiff-beaten egg whites
1 cup whipping cream, whipped
1 *baked* 9-inch pastry shell

Soften gelatin in cold water. In saucepan, combine syrup, egg yolks, and salt. Cook, stirring constantly, till slightly thick. Remove from heat and add gelatin; stir to dissolve. Add vanilla. Chill till partially set. Beat till light and fluffy, and caramel-colored. Fold in egg whites, then whipped cream. Chill till mixture mounds. Pile into cooled pastry shell. Chill till firm.

Orange Chiffon Pie is refreshingly tangy, yet creamy rich—lemon sharpens the flavor while whipping cream adds a fluffy richness.

## COTTAGE CHEESE CHIFFON PIE

Combine 1½ cups fine zwieback crumbs and ½ cup melted butter or margarine; reserve ¼ cup of mixture. Pat remaining mixture onto bottom and sides of 9-inch pie plate; chill.

Combine 1 envelope (1 tablespoon) unflavored gelatin, ⅔ cup sugar, and ½ teaspoon salt in saucepan. Blend in ½ cup milk and 2 slightly beaten egg yolks. Cook and stir over medium heat till mixture is slightly thickened. Remove from heat. Add 1½ cups small-curd cream-style cottage cheese, sieved, 1 teaspoon grated lemon peel, and 3 tablespoons lemon juice.

Beat 2 egg whites till soft peaks form. Gradually add ⅓ cup sugar; beat to stiff peaks. Fold into cottage cheese mixture. Fold in ½ cup whipping cream, whipped. Chill till mixture mounds. Pile into crust. Top with reserved crumbs. Chill till firm, about 4 to 5 hours.

## FLUFFY MANDARIN PIE

1 11-ounce can Mandarin oranges
1 envelope (1 tablespoon) unflavored
  gelatin
¼ cup sugar
2 slightly beaten egg yolks
¾ cup milk
1 teaspoon grated lemon peel
1 teaspoon lemon juice
2 egg whites
¼ teaspoon salt
¼ cup sugar
½ cup whipping cream, whipped
1 *baked* 9-inch pastry shell

Drain oranges, reserving ½ cup syrup; dice oranges, reserving a few for garnish. Combine gelatin and ¼ cup sugar; add reserved syrup, egg yolks, and milk. Cook and stir till mixture comes to boil; reduce heat and cook 1 minute. Add lemon peel and juice. Chill till partially thickened. Beat egg whites with salt till soft peaks form. Gradually add ¼ cup sugar, beating to stiff peaks. Fold egg whites, whipped cream, and diced oranges into gelatin mixture. Pile into cooled pastry shell. Garnish with reserved orange segments. Chill till firm.

32

## BLACK BOTTOM PIE

*Guests will rave about the fudge and French vanilla flavor combination of this special occasion treat—*

½ cup sugar
1 tablespoon cornstarch
2 cups milk, scalded
4 beaten egg yolks
1 teaspoon vanilla
1 6-ounce package (1 cup) semisweet
   chocolate pieces
1 *baked* 9-inch pastry shell

• • •

1 envelope (1 tablespoon) unflavored
   gelatin
¼ cup cold water
½ teaspoon rum extract *or* 2 tablespoons
   rum
4 egg whites
½ cup sugar

Combine first 2 ingredients. Slowly add milk to egg yolks. Stir in sugar mixture. Cook and stir over medium heat till custard thickens and coats spoon. Remove from heat; add vanilla. Stir *1 cup* custard with chocolate pieces till melted. Pour into cooled pastry shell; chill.

Soften gelatin in water; add to remaining hot custard; stir till dissolved. Stir in rum extract. Chill till slightly thickened. Beat egg whites till soft peaks form; gradually add sugar and beat to stiff peaks. Fold in custard. Pile over chocolate layer; chill till set. Garnish top of pie with chopped California walnuts.

## LEMON CHIFFON PIE

In saucepan, combine 1 envelope (1 tablespoon) unflavored gelatin, ½ cup sugar, and ½ teaspoon salt. Beat together 4 egg yolks, ⅓ cup lemon juice, and ⅔ cup water. Stir into gelatin mixture. Cook and stir over medium heat just till mixture comes to boiling. Remove from heat and stir in 1 teaspoon grated lemon peel. Chill, stirring occasionally, till mixture is partially set.

Beat 4 egg whites till soft peaks form. Gradually add ½ cup sugar, beating till stiff peaks form. Fold in gelatin mixture. Fold in ½ cup whipping cream, whipped. Pile filling into cooled *baked* 9-inch pastry shell; chill till firm. Garnish with dollops of additional whipped cream and sprigs of fresh mint, if desired.

## PUMPKIN CHIFFON PIE

1 envelope unflavored gelatin
½ cup sugar
½ teaspoon salt
½ teaspoon cinnamon
½ teaspoon allspice
¼ teaspoon ginger
¼ teaspoon nutmeg
¾ cup milk
2 slightly beaten egg yolks
1 cup canned pumpkin
2 egg whites
¼ cup sugar
½ cup whipping cream, whipped
1 9-inch graham-cracker crust

Combine first 7 ingredients in saucepan. Stir in milk, egg yolks, and pumpkin. Cook and stir over medium heat till mixture boils and gelatin dissolves. Remove from heat and chill till partially set. Beat egg whites till soft peaks form; gradually add sugar and beat to stiff peaks. Fold into pumpkin mixture with whipped cream. Pile into crust. Chill till firm. Trim with whipped cream and California walnut halves.

## DAIQUIRI PIE

1 envelope unflavored gelatin
1 cup sugar
¼ teaspoon salt
⅓ cup lime juice
⅓ cup water
3 well beaten egg yolks
½ teaspoon grated lime peel
2 drops green food coloring
¼ cup light rum
3 egg whites
⅓ cup sugar
1 *baked* 9-inch pastry shell

In saucepan, combine first 3 ingredients. Add lime juice and water. Stir in egg yolks, mix well. Cook and stir over low heat till mixture boils and gelatin dissolves. Remove from heat; add lime peel and food coloring. Cool to room temperature; stir in rum. Chill till mixture is partially set. Beat egg whites to soft peaks. Gradually add sugar; beat to stiff peaks. Fold in gelatin mixture. Chill till mixture mounds. Pile into cooled shell. Chill till firm. Top with whipped cream and candy lime slices, if desired.

## CHOCOLATE CHIFFON PIE

1 envelope (1 tablespoon) unflavored
   gelatin
1 cup sugar
1 cup milk
2 1-ounce squares unsweetened chocolate
2 2-ounce packages dessert topping mix
   *or* 2 cups whipping cream
1 *baked* 9-inch pastry shell

Combine gelatin, sugar, and dash salt in sauce-pan. Add milk; cut chocolate in small pieces and add. Cook and stir over medium heat till gelatin is dissolved and chocolate is melted. (Mixture will be chocolate flecked.) Chill, stirring occasionally, till mixture mounds. Prepare dessert topping mix according to package directions or whip cream. Fold into gelatin mixture. Pile into cooled pastry shell. Chill till firm. If desired, trim with additional whipped cream and Chocolate Curls (see index).

## RASPBERRY CHIFFON PIE

1 10-ounce package frozen red
   raspberries, thawed
1 3-ounce package raspberry-flavored
   gelatin
¾ cup boiling water
2 tablespoons lemon juice
½ cup whipping cream, whipped
Dash salt
2 egg whites
¼ cup sugar
1 *baked* 9-inch pastry shell

Drain raspberries; add water to syrup to make ⅔ cup. Dissolve gelatin in boiling water; add lemon juice and raspberry syrup. Chill till partially set. Beat till soft peaks form. Fold in raspberries and whipped cream. Add dash salt to egg whites; beat till soft peaks form. Add sugar gradually; beat to stiff peaks. Fold into raspberry mixture. Pile into cooled pastry shell; chill.

This rainbow of glamorous chiffon pies includes Pumpkin Chiffon, Daiquiri Pie, Raspberry Chiffon, and Chocolate Chiffon. Round out the party with piping-hot coffee.

## PINK PARTY PIE

1 cup boiling water
1 3-ounce package strawberry-flavored
   gelatin
2 tablespoons sugar
1 10-ounce package frozen sliced
   strawberries, broken in chunks
½ cup whipping cream, whipped
1 *baked* 9-inch pastry shell

In blender, put water, gelatin, and sugar; cover and blend at high speed about 10 seconds or till gelatin and sugar are dissolved. Add berries; cover and blend about 15 to 20 seconds or till thoroughly mixed. Chill till almost set. Blend mixture at high speed about 1 minute or till frothy. Pour into mixing bowl; chill till mixture mounds. Fold in whipped cream. Pile into pastry shell. Chill 3 hours or till firm. Garnish with dollops of additional whipped cream.

## STRAWBERRY PETAL PIE

Pastry for 9-inch single crust pie
1 envelope (1 tablespoon) unflavored
   gelatin
¼ cup sugar
1 cup orange juice
2 tablespoons lemon juice
3 slightly beaten egg yolks
1 teaspoon grated orange peel
3 egg whites
¼ cup sugar
1 pint fresh strawberries, sliced

Fit pastry into pie plate; trim even with edge. From remaining dough, cut 1-inch circles. Moisten rim of pie shell with water; place circles on rim, overlapping slightly. Press each circle with fork to seal in place. Prick well. Bake at 450° for 10 to 12 minutes; cool.

Combine gelatin, sugar, and dash salt in saucepan; stir in orange and lemon juices and egg yolks. Cook and stir over medium heat just till mixture comes to a boil. Remove from heat; add orange peel. Chill till partially set. Beat egg whites till soft peaks form; gradually add sugar, beating to stiff peaks. Fold in gelatin mixture. Spread *half* the filling in pastry shell; top with *1 cup* strawberries. Pile in remaining filling and top with remaining strawberries. Chill 2 to 3 hours. Top with mounds of whipped cream.

## SEAFOAM CANTALOUPE PIE

1 envelope (1 tablespoon) unflavored
   gelatin
½ cup sugar
¼ teaspoon salt
4 slightly beaten egg yolks
½ cup lime juice
¼ cup water
1 teaspoon grated lime peel
Few drops green food coloring
4 egg whites
½ cup sugar
½ cup whipping cream, whipped
1½ cups cantaloupe balls
1 *baked* 9-inch pastry shell

Combine gelatin, ½ cup sugar, and salt. Stir together egg yolks, lime juice, and water; add to gelatin mixture. Cook and stir over medium heat just till mixture comes to a boil. Remove from heat; add lime peel and food coloring. Chill, stirring occasionally, till mixture mounds.

Beat egg whites to soft peaks; gradually add ½ cup sugar; beat to stiff peaks. Fold in gelatin mixture. Fold in whipped cream and cantaloupe. Pile into cooled pastry shell. Chill till firm. Top with a wreath of additional whipped cream and toasted coconut.

## PEACH BLUSH PIE

Drain one 1-pound 13-ounce can (3½ cups) sliced peaches, reserving syrup. Mix ½ cup sugar, 1 envelope (1 tablespoon) unflavored gelatin, ¼ teaspoon salt, and *1 cup of reserved syrup*. Heat and stir till gelatin dissolves. Add ¼ cup lemon juice and few drops almond extract. Chill till partially set.

Add 2 egg whites; beat till fluffy. Let stand till mixture mounds slightly. Reserve a few peaches for trim; dice remainder and fold in along with ½ cup whipping cream, whipped, and 2 tablespoons finely chopped candied ginger. Pile into cooled *baked* 9-inch pastry shell. Top with reserved peaches. Chill. Spoon Glaze over top. Chill till set.

*Glaze:* Mix 1 tablespoon sugar, 2 teaspoons cornstarch, dash salt, and remaining peach syrup. Cook and stir till mixture boils; cook 2 minutes. Add 1 teaspoon lemon juice, few drops almond extract, and 1 drop red food coloring. Cool to room temperature.

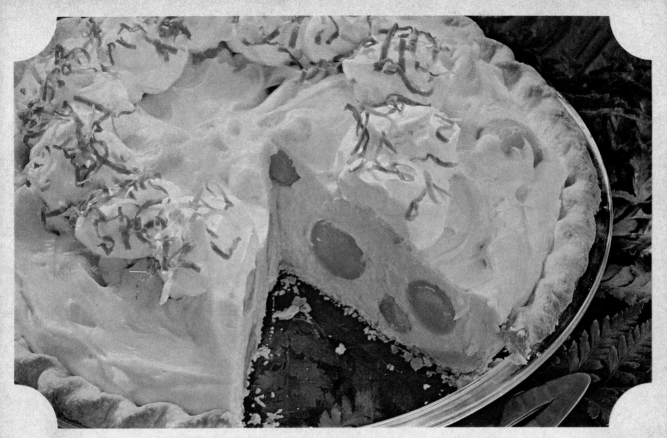

Cloud-light lime filling and cantaloupe balls make this Sea-foam Cantaloupe Pie as cool a summer dessert as you can find. Make it your standby for summer entertaining.

## PEACH-BERRY PIE

Combine 1½ cups diced fresh peaches, ½ cup fresh or frozen raspberries, and ½ cup sugar; let stand 30 minutes. Drain, reserving syrup. Dissolve one 3-ounce package lemon-flavored gelatin in 1 cup boiling water; cool. Add fruit syrup, ⅛ teaspoon almond extract, and dash salt. Chill till partially set; fold in fruit and ½ cup whipping cream, whipped. Pile into 9-inch vanilla-wafer crust. Chill.

## PEACH CHIFFON PIE

Sprinkle 3 cups sliced fresh peaches with ½ cup sugar; set aside. Soften 1 envelope (1 table-spoon) unflavored gelatin in 1¼ cups cold water; dissolve over low heat; cool. Drain syrup from peaches; stir into gelatin mixture. Chill till partially set; beat till fluffy. Fold in peaches and ½ cup whipping cream, whipped. Pile into *baked* 9-inch pastry shell; chill.

## GINGER FRUIT PIE

1 cup fine gingersnap crumbs
3 tablespoons butter or margarine, melted
2 cups miniature marshmallows *or* 20 large marshmallows
2 tablespoons milk
1 3-ounce package cream cheese, softened
1 cup dairy sour cream
1 teaspoon vanilla
Dash salt
1 1-pound can (2 cups) fruit cocktail, drained

For crust, combine crumbs and melted butter; press onto bottom and sides of 9-inch pie plate. Chill while making filling.

Melt marshmallows with milk in double boiler, stirring occasionally; cool 10 minutes. Combine cheese, sour cream, vanilla, and salt; beat smooth. Stir in marshmallow mixture and fruit cocktail. Pile into crust. Chill till firm, about 5 hours. Trim with additional fruit.

# PEPPERMINT CHIFFON PIE

Mix ½ cup crushed peppermint-stick candy, ¼ cup sugar, 1 envelope (1 tablespoon) unflavored gelatin, 1¼ cups milk, 3 slightly beaten egg yolks, and ¼ teaspoon salt in saucepan. Cook and stir over low heat till gelatin dissolves and candy melts. Tint with 4 or 5 drops red food coloring. Chill till partially set.

Beat 3 egg whites till soft peaks form; gradually add ¼ cup sugar, beating to stiff peaks. Fold in gelatin mixture. Fold in ½ cup whipping cream, whipped. Chill till mixture mounds slightly; pile into *baked* 9-inch pastry shell. Chill till firm. Trim with whipped cream.

# LAZY GRASSHOPPER PIE

Make one 3¾-ounce package vanilla whipped dessert mix according to package directions. Stir in 2 tablespoons green creme de menthe and 1 tablespoon white creme de cocoa. Chill till mixture mounds slightly. Pile into *baked* 8-inch pastry shell. Chill. Trim with whipped dessert topping and chocolate curls.

# FESTIVE EGGNOG PIE

1 envelope (1 tablespoon) unflavored
  gelatin
2 tablespoons sugar
¼ teaspoon salt
1¾ cups milk
3 slightly beaten egg yolks
1 teaspoon rum flavoring
3 egg whites
¼ cup sugar
½ cup thinly sliced candied cherries
1 *baked* 9-inch pastry shell
½ cup whipping cream, whipped

Mix gelatin, 2 tablespoons sugar, and salt in saucepan. Add milk and egg yolks. Cook and stir over low heat till gelatin dissolves and mixture thickens slightly. Add flavoring. Chill, stirring occasionally, till partially set. Beat egg whites till soft peaks form; gradually add ¼ cup sugar, beating to stiff peaks. Fold in gelatin mixture with cherries. Chill till mixture mounds slightly. Pile into cooled pastry shell. Chill till firm. Spread with whipped cream. Trim with additional cherries and Brazil nut slices.

# PEANUT-BUTTER CHIFFON PIE

2 *teaspoons* unflavored gelatin
¼ cup sugar
¼ teaspoon salt
½ teaspoon nutmeg
1 cup water
½ cup peanut butter
2 slightly beaten egg yolks
1 teaspoon vanilla
2 egg whites
2 tablespoons sugar
½ cup whipping cream, whipped
1 fully ripe banana
1 *baked* 9-inch pastry shell

Mix first 4 ingredients. Slowly add water to peanut butter in saucepan; blend smooth; stir in egg yolks. Add gelatin mixture. Cook and stir till mixture thickens slightly. Add vanilla. Chill till partially set. Beat egg whites to soft peaks; gradually add 2 tablespoons sugar, beating to stiff peaks. Fold into gelatin mixture. Fold in whipped cream. Slice banana into pastry shell. Top with filling. Chill till firm.

# PECAN CHIFFON TARTS

1 envelope (1 tablespoon) unflavored
  gelatin
⅓ cup brown sugar
½ teaspoon salt
4 beaten egg yolks
¾ cup milk
1 teaspoon vanilla
4 egg whites
⅓ cup brown sugar
Butter-browned Pecans
8 *baked* 4-inch tart shells

Combine gelatin, ⅓ cup brown sugar, and salt in top of double boiler. Add egg yolks and milk. Cook and stir over boiling water till mixture thickens slightly. Remove from heat; add vanilla. Chill, stirring occasionally, till the mixture mounds slightly. Beat egg whites till soft peaks form; gradually add ⅓ cup brown sugar, beating to stiff peaks. Fold in gelatin mixture, then *half* the Butter-browned Pecans. Pile into tart shells. Chill till firm. Top with remaining pecans.

*Butter-browned Pecans:* Toast 1 cup chopped pecans in 2 tablespoons butter or margarine in skillet, stirring frequently. Drain; cool.

# CHILLY PARFAIT AND FROZEN PIES

## STRAWBERRY SUNSHINE PIE

1 *baked* 9-inch pastry shell
1 pint lemon sherbet, softened
1 recipe Meringue (3 egg whites)
1 quart fresh strawberries, sliced and
    sweetened with 1 tablespoon sugar

Spread sherbet in bottom of pastry shell; freeze solid, 4 to 5 hours or overnight. Prepare meringue (see index). Remove pie from freezer. Working quickly, arrange strawberries over sherbet. Spread meringue over berries, being careful to seal to edge of pastry. Place pie on cutting board and bake in very hot oven (475°) till golden, 5 to 6 minutes. With sharp knife dipped in water, cut in wedges and serve immediately.

## NEAPOLITAN ICE CREAM PIE

Spread 1 pint chocolate ice cream, softened, in bottom of *baked* 9-inch pastry shell. Top with 1 pint strawberry ice cream, softened. Freeze solid, 4 to 5 hours. Remove from freezer. Spread 1 recipe Meringue (3 egg whites—see index) over ice cream, sealing to edge of pastry. Place pie on cutting board and bake at 475° for 4 to 5 minutes or till meringue is golden. Cut in wedges; drizzle with Chocolate Sauce. Serve at once.

*Chocolate Sauce:* Heat and stir 4 squares (4 ounces) unsweetened chocolate and ¾ cup water over low heat till melted. Add 1 cup sugar and dash salt. Simmer till slightly thickened, about 5 minutes. Remove from heat; blend in 6 tablespoons butter and 1 teaspoon vanilla.

A variation of famous baked Alaska, Strawberry Sunshine Pie is a dazzler. Lemon sherbet and fresh strawberries will stay cool under fluffy meringue while the meringue browns.

## PUMPKIN PARFAIT PIE

½ cup brown sugar
4 *teaspoons* unflavored gelatin
1 teaspoon instant coffee powder
½ teaspoon ginger
½ teaspoon cinnamon
¼ teaspoon nutmeg
1 cup boiling water
1 pint vanilla ice cream
1 cup canned pumpkin
1 9-inch graham-cracker crust

Blend brown sugar, gelatin, coffee powder, and spices in mixing bowl; add boiling water; stir to dissolve. Add ice cream by spoonfuls, stirring till melted. Stir in pumpkin. Chill till mixture mounds, about 5 minutes. Pile into crumb crust; chill till firm.

## LIME PARFAIT PIE

*The perfect ending for a perfect meal—*

2 3-ounce packages *or* 1 6-ounce package
  lime-flavored gelatin
2 cups boiling water
1 teaspoon shredded lime peel
⅓ cup lime juice
1 quart vanilla ice cream
1 *baked* 10-inch pastry shell

Dissolve gelatin in boiling water. Stir in lime peel and juice. Add ice cream by spoonfuls, stirring till melted. Chill till mixture mounds. Pile into pastry shell. Chill till firm. Top with whipped cream and maraschino cherries.

## STRAWBERRY FROZEN PIE

1 8-ounce package cream cheese, softened
1 cup dairy sour cream
2 10-ounce packages frozen sliced
  strawberries, thawed
1 9-inch graham-cracker crust

Blend cream cheese and sour cream. Reserve ½ cup berries (and syrup); add remaining berries and syrup to cheese mixture. Pour into crust. Freeze firm. Remove from freezer 5 minutes before serving. Cut in wedges; serve topped with reserved berries in syrup.

## PINEAPPLE PARFAIT PIE

1 8¾-ounce can crushed pineapple
1 3-ounce package lemon-flavored gelatin
2 tablespoons lemon juice
1 pint vanilla ice cream
1 9-inch vanilla-wafer crust

Drain pineapple. Add enough water to syrup to make 1 cup; heat to boiling. Add to gelatin and stir till dissolved. Add ¼ cup cold water and the lemon juice. Add ice cream by spoonfuls, stirring till melted. Chill till mixture mounds; fold in pineapple. Pile into crust. Chill till firm. Trim with whipped cream and pineapple slices.

## CHERRY BURGUNDY PIE

1 1-pound can pitted dark sweet cherries
1 3-ounce package cherry-flavored gelatin
1 pint vanilla ice cream
1 teaspoon lemon juice
3 tablespoons red Burgundy wine
1 *baked* 8-inch pastry shell

Drain cherries, reserving syrup. Add enough water to syrup to make 1 cup; heat to boiling. Dissolve gelatin in boiling liquid. Add ice cream by spoonfuls, stirring till melted. Blend in lemon juice and wine. Chill till mixture mounds. Quarter cherries; fold into mixture. Chill again, if necessary, before piling into shell. Chill till firm. Trim with whipped cream.

## GINGERED ICE CREAM PIE

1 pint vanilla ice cream
1 to 2 tablespoons finely chopped
  candied ginger
1 *baked* 9-inch pastry shell
1 cup canned pumpkin
1 cup sugar
½ teaspoon salt
½ teaspoon ginger
¼ teaspoon nutmeg
1½ cups miniature marshmallows
1 cup whipping cream, whipped

Stir ice cream just to soften; fold in ginger; spread over bottom of pastry shell. Freeze firm. Mix pumpkin with next 5 ingredients; fold in whipped cream. Pile over ice cream layer. Freeze.

## PEANUT ICE CREAM PIE

Prepare 9-inch graham-cracker crust; reserve 1 to 2 tablespoons crumbs for garnish. Chill.

Soften 1 quart vanilla ice cream. Fold in ½ cup crunchy peanut butter, then fold in ½ cup whipping cream, whipped. Quickly spoon mixture into crust. Sprinkle reserved crumbs around edge. Freeze till firm, about 5 hours. Remove from freezer 10 to 15 minutes before serving.

## FROZEN LEMON FLUFF PIE

2 egg yolks
2 tablespoons sugar
1½ teaspoons grated lemon peel
3 tablespoons lemon juice
¼ teaspoon salt
½ cup whipping cream, whipped

• • •

2 egg whites
¼ cup sugar
1 9-inch graham-cracker crust

Beat egg yolks; gradually add 2 tablespoons sugar; beat till thick and lemon-colored. Stir in lemon peel, juice, and salt. Fold in whipped cream. Beat egg whites till soft peaks form; gradually add ¼ cup sugar, beating till stiff peaks form. Fold in lemon mixture. Spoon into crust; freeze. Garnish with whipped cream.

## FUDGE RIBBON PIE

Spread 1 pint softened vanilla ice cream in 1 *baked* 9-inch pastry shell; cover with *half* the cooled Fudge Sauce; freeze. Repeat layers with another pint vanilla ice cream and remaining Fudge Sauce. Freeze overnight.

Prepare 1 recipe Meringue (3 egg whites—see Index). Fold 3 tablespoons crushed peppermint-stick candy into meringue. Remove pie from freezer. Spread meringue over chocolate layer; being careful to seal to edge. Sprinkle top with 1 tablespoon crushed peppermint-stick candy. Place pie on cutting board; bake at 475° for 5 to 6 minutes, or till golden. Serve at once.

*Fudge Sauce:* Mix 2 tablespoons butter or margarine, two 1-ounce squares unsweetened chocolate, 1 cup sugar, and one 6-ounce can (⅔ cup) evaporated milk in saucepan. Cook and stir till thick. Add 1 teaspoon vanilla. Cool.

## PINK APPLE PIE ALASKA

*Apple pie a la mode under a pink cloud of meringue. It can be made ahead and finished just at serving time—*

2 cups sugar
2 cups water
⅓ cup red cinnamon candies
½ teaspoon red food coloring
4 medium apples, pared, cored, and sliced (about 4 cups)
1 *baked* 9-inch pastry shell
1 quart vanilla ice cream, softened
3 egg whites
6 tablespoons sugar
Red food coloring

Combine 2 cups sugar, water, cinnamon candies, and ½ teaspoon red food coloring. Heat till candies are dissolved. Add apple slices and cook till apples are tender. Remove from heat and let stand till apples are desired color; drain and cool. Line bottom and sides of cooled pastry shell with apple slices. Spread ice cream over apples; freeze for several hours.

Beat egg whites to soft peaks. Gradually add sugar, beating till stiff peaks form. Add enough food coloring to tint meringue pink. Spread over ice cream, sealing to pastry. Place on board; brown lightly at 475° for 5 to 6 minutes.

## PIE CUES

Good equipment makes any job easier. A well-equipped cook needs a pastry blender, rolling pin with stockinette, and pastry cloth. A pastry wheel is handy, too.

Your pie will have a beautiful, golden-brown edge if protected with an aluminum foil collar for part of the baking. Fold a 2½-inch strip around the rim, making sure the foil covers all the fluted edge.

Before cutting a meringue-topped pie, dip the knife in water. (No need to dry it off.) Repeat whenever meringue sticks.

For a non-stick crumb crust, wrap a hot wet towel under the bottom and around the sides of the pie plate just before serving the pie. Hold the towel against the plate for a few minutes. This loosens the crust so that each piece of pie slips out easily.

# SHELLS AND CRUSTS

Sprinkle few drops water at a time over flour mixture; toss with fork. Then push moistened part aside.

For perfect pastry circles, press dough with edge of hand 3 times across in both directions; then roll.

Flute edge by pressing dough with forefinger against wedge made of finger and thumb of other hand.

Cut slits in top crust. Lift the pastry by rolling it over rolling pin; then unroll over the well-filled pie.

## PLAIN PASTRY

*For one single-crust pie or 4 to 6 tart shells:*

1½ cups sifted all-purpose flour
½ teaspoon salt
½ cup shortening
4 to 5 tablespoons cold water

*For one 8-, 9-, or 10-inch double-crust or lattice-top pie, two 8-, 9-, or 10-inch single-crust pies, or 6 to 8 tart shells:*

2 cups sifted all-purpose flour
1 teaspoon salt
⅔ cup shortening
5 to 7 tablespoons cold water

Sift together flour and salt; cut in shortening with pastry blender or blending fork till pieces are the size of small peas. (For extra tender pastry, cut in *half* the shortening till mixture looks like cornmeal. Then cut in remaining till like small peas.) Sprinkle 1 tablespoon water over part of mixture. Gently toss with fork; push to side of bowl. Sprinkle next tablespoon water over dry part; mix lightly; push to moistened part at side. Repeat till all is moistened. Form into ball. (For double-crust and lattice-top pies, divide dough for lower and upper crust. Form each portion into ball.) Flatten ball on lightly floured surface. Roll from center to edge till dough is ⅛ inch thick.

*To bake single-crust pie shells:* Fit pastry into pie plate, trim ½ to 1 inch beyond edge; fold under and flute. Prick bottom and sides well with fork. Bake in a very hot oven (450°) for 10 to 12 minutes or till golden.

*For lattice-top pie:* Trim lower crust ½ inch beyond edge of pie plate. Roll remaining dough ⅛ inch thick. Cut strips of pastry ½ to ¾ inch wide with pastry wheel or knife. Lay strips on filled pie at 1-inch intervals. Fold back alternate strips as you weave cross-strips. Trim lattice even with outer rim of pie plate; fold lower crust over strips. Seal and flute.

*For double-crust pie:* Trim lower crust even with rim of pie plate. Cut slits in upper crust. Fit loosely over filling; trim ½ inch beyond edge; tuck under edge of lower crust. Flute.

## ELECTRIC MIXER PASTRY

*For one 8- or 9-inch single-crust pie:*

Measure ¼ cup cold water, ½ cup shortening, 1¼ cups instant-type flour, and ½ teaspoon salt into small mixing bowl. Mix at lowest speed on electric mixer till dough begins to form, 15 to 30 seconds. Shape into a firm ball. Flatten; smooth edges. Flour generously on both sides with instant-type flour. Roll out on well-floured surface to ⅛ inch. Fit into pie plate; trim pastry and flute edge. Prick bottom and sides well. Bake at 450° for 10 to 12 minutes or till golden.

## OIL PASTRY

*For one 8- or 9-inch double-crust pie:*

Sift together 2 cups sifted all-purpose flour and 1½ teaspoons salt. Pour ½ cup salad oil and 4 to 5 tablespoons cold water or milk into measuring cup (do not stir). Add all at once to flour mixture. Stir lightly with fork. Form into 2 balls; flatten slightly.

Roll each between two 12-inch squares of waxed paper. When dough is rolled to edges of paper, it will be right thickness for crust. Peel off top sheet of paper and fit dough, paper side up into pie plate. Remove paper. Finish pie following directions for double-crust pie.

## COCONUT CRUST

Combine one 3½-ounce can (1⅓ cups) flaked coconut and 2 tablespoons melted butter or margarine. Press into 9-inch pie plate. Bake at (325°) for 15 minutes, or till light golden brown.

## VANILLA-WAFER CRUST

Mix together 1½ cups fine vanilla-wafer crumbs and 6 tablespoons melted butter or margarine. Press firmly into a 9-inch pie plate. Chill.

## CHOCOLATE-WAFER CRUST

Mix together 1½ cups fine chocolate-wafer crumbs and 6 tablespoons melted butter or margarine. Press firmly into 9-inch pie plate. Chill.

## GINGERSNAP CRUST

Mix 1½ cups fine gingersnap crumbs and ¼ cup softened butter or margarine. Press firmly into buttered 9-inch pie plate. Bake in moderate oven (375°) about 8 minutes. Cool.

## ZWIEBACK CRUST

Mix 1 cup zwieback crumbs, ¼ cup confectioners' sugar, and 2 tablespoons melted butter or margarine. Press into buttered 8-inch pie plate. Chill till set.

For **GRAHAM-CRACKER CRUST:** Combine 1¼ cups fine graham-cracker crumbs, ¼ cup sugar, and 6 tablespoons melted butter or margarine; mix. Press firmly into 9-inch pie plate. Bake at 375° for 6 to 8 minutes or till edges are browned; cool. For unbaked crust chill 45 minutes; fill.

*Test Kitchen tip:* Heap crumbs in 9-inch pie plate; press 8-inch pie plate into crumbs. Crust will shape itself evenly.

Freeze pies before baking (no slits in top crust). A 2½-inch cardboard collar protects crust. Wrap in moisture-vapor-proof material; seal; label. Bake frozen pies without thawing. Cut slits in top crust after 5 minutes of baking; return to oven till browned.

# PICTURE PERFECT PIES

Lattice trick—place seven ½-inch pastry strips across filling. Weave first cross strip through center. Fold back alternate strips each time you add a cross strip.

A pastry wheel cuts the zigzag edges of the lattice strips. After sealing lower crust over lattice, take a shortcut by impressing double row of scallops with teaspoon.

For twisted lattice, twist ¾-inch strips as you place them on filling. Place cross strips diagonally, twisting as you weave.

Cut pastry petals with doughnut "hole" cutter bent in shape of leaf. Overlap petals on moistened rim of pie, pressing in place.

To seal in juice, fold trimmed lower crust over pastry strips. Flute a high, pretty edge by pressing with fingers as shown here.

Fancy spiral can be done in a jiffy. Moisten and join ends of ¾-inch pastry strips to make long strip. Twist and swirl atop pie.

Trim crust even with rim; moisten edge. Loosely interlace two pastry strips around rim, pressing lower strip against rim at each crossover. Keep strips flat; don't stretch.

Snowflake center was cut with cooky cutter. Crust trim is made by pressing with beverage can opener, curved side down. Sprinkle top crust lightly with sugar for sparkle.

Trim crust even with rim; moisten edge. Press end of long ¾-inch strip to rim. Twist strip; press spiral to rim with left hand.

Trim crusts ½ inch beyond edge; pinch together. Cut scallops with tip of teaspoon; mark with fork. Brush the top with cream.

Trim pastry ½ to 1 inch beyond edge; fold under. Press dough forward diagonally with bent finger while pulling back with thumb.

Using a pastry tube, pipe on meringue in 4 rows. Pipe on 4 more rows to make diamond-shaped "windows." Brown in oven or broiler.

# PERFECT CAKES

Cakes move in happy social circles. What birthday party or wedding reception would be complete without a cake. At graduation parties and anniversary celebrations, bridal showers and neighborhood coffees, we spotlight cake, too. No food triumph makes a woman prouder than serving a beautiful cake, light and tender, delicately flavored and evenly grained. It can be the achievement of anyone who carefully follows a few simple rules.

Success in cake baking is not due to good luck or to a special touch for baking. Success results from accurate measuring and proper mixing, from using the technique best for the kinds and portions of ingredients, and from correct baking. In short, success is due to following a good recipe to the letter. Anyone can use these Better Homes and Gardens tested recipes with confidence.

**Toasted Butter Pecan Cake has rich flavor and the look of a special occasion, saying, "Let's celebrate."**

# WONDERFUL CHOCOLATE CAKES

## MOTHER'S BEST FUDGE CAKE

⅔ cup sugar
½ cup milk
1 slightly beaten egg
3 1-ounce squares unsweetened chocolate
½ cup shortening
1 cup sugar
1 teaspoon vanilla
2 eggs
2 cups sifted cake flour
1 teaspoon soda
½ teaspoon salt
1 cup milk

In saucepan combine first 4 ingredients. Cook and stir over medium heat till chocolate melts and mixture comes just to boiling. Cool. Gradually add 1 cup sugar to shortening, creaming till fluffy. Add vanilla. Add remaining eggs, one at a time, beating well after each.

Sift together dry ingredients. Add to creamed mixture alternately with 1 cup milk, beating just till smooth after each addition. Blend in the cooled chocolate mixture.

Bake in 2 greased and lightly floured 9x1½-inch round pans at 350° for 25 to 30 minutes or till done. Cool 10 minutes before removing from pans. Cool; frost and fill with Chocolate Frosting. Decorate with chocolate curls.

## COCOA FUDGE CAKE

Cream ¾ cup butter. Gradually add 1½ cups sugar, creaming till light. Add 3 egg yolks, one at a time, beating well after each. Add 1½ teaspoons vanilla and 1 teaspoon red food coloring. Sift together 2¼ cups sifted cake flour, ½ cup cocoa (regular-type, dry), and 3 teaspoons baking powder. Add to creamed mixture alternately with 1 cup cold water, beating just till mixture is smooth after each addition. Gently fold in 3 stiff-beaten egg whites.

Bake in 2 greased and lightly floured 9x1½-inch round pans at 350° for about 25 minutes. Cool 10 minutes before removing from pans. Cool; frost and fill with Chocolate Frosting.

Mother's Best Fudge Cake is a deep, dark chocolate cake with a velvety texture. It's crowned with a creamy chocolate frosting and decorated with chocolate curls for a triple chocolate treat in every forkful.

# SWEET CHOCOLATE CAKE

    1 4-ounce bar sweet cooking chocolate
    ⅓ cup water
    ½ cup butter or margarine
    1 cup sugar
    3 egg yolks
    1 teaspoon vanilla
    1¾ cups sifted cake flour
    1 teaspoon soda
    ½ teaspoon salt
    ⅔ cup buttermilk
    3 stiff-beaten egg whites
    Coconut Pecan Frosting

Combine chocolate and ⅓ cup water; stir over low heat till chocolate melts; cool. Cream butter; gradually add sugar, creaming till light. Add egg yolks, one at a time, beating well after each. Add vanilla and chocolate; mix well.

Sift together dry ingredients; add to creamed mixture alternately with buttermilk, beating after each addition. Fold in egg whites. Bake in 2 greased and lightly floured 8x1½-inch round pans in moderate oven (350°) about 35 minutes or till done. Cool 10 minutes before removing from pans. Spread Coconut Pecan Frosting between cooled layers and on top of cake.

*Coconut Pecan Frosting:* Combine one 6-ounce can (⅔ cup) evaporated milk or light cream, ⅔ cup sugar, ¼ cup butter, 1 slightly beaten egg, and dash salt in saucepan. Cook over medium heat, stirring constantly, till mixture thickens and begins to boil, about 12 minutes. Cool slightly. Stir in 1 teaspoon vanilla. Add one 3½-ounce can (1⅓ cups) flaked coconut and ½ cup chopped pecans. Cool thoroughly.

# SPICED CHOCOLATE CAKE

Place ⅔ cup shortening in mixing bowl. Sift in 2 cups sifted all-purpose flour, 2 cups sugar, 1 teaspoon baking powder, 1 teaspoon soda, 1 teaspoon salt, 1 teaspoon cloves, 1 teaspoon cinnamon, and 1 teaspoon instant coffee powder. Add 1 cup buttermilk; mix till all flour is moistened. Beat vigorously 2 minutes. Stir in ½ cup buttermilk, 3 eggs, four 1-ounce squares unsweetened chocolate, melted and cooled, and 1 teaspoon vanilla. Beat 2 minutes longer. Bake in greased and lightly floured 13x9x2-inch baking dish in moderate oven (350°) 40 minutes or till done. Cool. Frost with Seven Minute Frosting.

# RED DEVIL'S FOOD CAKE

    ½ cup shortening
    1 cup sugar
    3 egg yolks
    1 teaspoon vanilla
    2½ cups sifted cake flour
    ½ cup cocoa (regular-type, dry)
    1½ teaspoons soda
    1 teaspoon salt
    1⅓ cups cold water
    3 egg whites
    ¾ cup sugar

Cream shortening and 1 cup sugar till light and fluffy. Add egg yolks, one at a time, beating well after each. Stir in vanilla. Sift together cake flour, cocoa, soda, and salt; add to creamed mixture alternately with cold water, beating well after each addition.

Beat egg whites till soft peaks form; gradually add ¾ cup sugar, beating till stiff peaks form. Fold into batter; blend well. Bake in 2 greased and lightly floured 8x1½-inch round pans in moderate oven (350°) about 35 to 40 minutes or till cake tests done. Cool 10 minutes; remove from pans. Cool; frost with Chocolate Frosting.

# SOUR CREAM CHOCO CAKE

    ½ cup shortening
    2 cups sifted cake flour
    2 cups sugar
    1 teaspoon soda
    ½ teaspoon salt
    ½ cup dairy sour cream
    ½ teaspoon vanilla
    1 cup water
    4 1-ounce squares unsweetened chocolate, melted and cooled
    2 eggs

Place shortening in large mixing bowl. Sift in flour, sugar, soda, and salt. Add sour cream, vanilla, and ⅔ cup water. Mix till flour is moistened. Beat vigorously 2 minutes, scraping bottom and sides of bowl often. Add chocolate, eggs, and *remaining* water; beat 2 minutes longer.

Bake in 2 greased and lightly floured 9x1½-inch round cake pans in moderate oven (350°) 25 to 30 minutes or till cake tests done. Cool 10 minutes; remove from pans. Cool; fill and frost with Penuche Frosting.

48

## CHOCOLATE LAYER CAKE

Cream ⅔ cup butter. Add 1¾ cups sugar gradually, creaming till light and fluffy; add 2 eggs, beating well after each. Stir in 1 teaspoon vanilla and two and one-half 1-ounce squares unsweetened chocolate, melted and cooled. Sift together 2½ cups sifted cake flour, 1¼ teaspoons soda, and ½ teaspoon salt. Add to creamed mixture alternately with 1¼ cups *icy cold* water. Beat after each addition. Bake in 2 greased and lightly floured 9x1½-inch round pans at 350° for 30 to 35 minutes or till done. Cool 10 minutes before removing from pans. Cool; frost with chocolate frosting prepared from a mix.

## CHOCOLATE DATE-NUT CAKE

2¼ cups sifted cake flour
1 cup sugar
3 teaspoons baking powder
1 teaspoon salt
1 cup milk
⅓ cup salad oil
1 teaspoon vanilla
½ 1-ounce square unsweetened
   chocolate, grated
2 egg yolks
2 egg whites
½ cup sugar
Date Nut Filling

Sift together in a large bowl the first 4 ingredients. Add milk, salad oil, vanilla, and chocolate. Beat 1 minute at medium speed of electric mixer, scraping sides and bottom of bowl often. Add egg yolks and beat 1 minute more at medium speed. Beat egg whites till soft peaks form; gradually add ½ cup sugar beating till stiff peaks form. Fold into chocolate mixture. Bake in a greased and lightly floured 13x9x2-inch baking pan in a moderate oven (350°) about 35 to 40 minutes or till cake tests done. Cool. Spread with Date Nut Filling and frost with Seven Minute Frosting.

*Date Nut Filling:* Combine 1 cup finely chopped dates, one 6-ounce can (⅔ cup) evaporated milk, ⅔ cup sugar, dash salt, and 2 slightly beaten egg yolks in saucepan. Cook and stir over medium heat till mixture is slightly thickened, about 5 minutes. Remove from heat. Add ½ cup chopped California walnuts and ½ teaspoon vanilla. Cool to room temperature.

## CHOCOLATE FUDGE CAKE

*Cake making has never been easier. Mix all ingredients at the same time in the cake pan—*

In a 9x9x2-inch pan, combine ⅓ cup salad oil (or melt ⅓ cup shortening; remove from heat and cool), 2 envelopes (2 ounces) no-melt unsweetened chocolate, 1 egg, 1 cup sugar, 1¼ cups instant-type flour, ½ teaspoon soda, ½ teaspoon salt, ½ teaspoon vanilla, and ¾ cup water. Beat with a fork till smooth and creamy, about 2 minutes. Scrape bottom and sides of pan with rubber spatula after 1 minute of beating. Spread batter evenly in pan; sprinkle with ½ cup semisweet chocolate pieces. Arrange 9 to 12 California walnut halves over top. Bake in moderate oven (350°) about 30 minutes or till cake springs back when touched in center. Cool.

## CALICO CRUMB CAKE

*Flavor will remind you of a hot fudge sundae—*

½ cup sifted all-purpose flour
½ cup brown sugar
¼ cup butter or margarine
½ cup finely chopped nuts
• • •
2 cups sifted all-purpose flour
1 cup granulated sugar
1 teaspoon soda
1 teaspoon salt
½ cup shortening
2 eggs
1 cup buttermilk *or* sour milk
2 teaspoons vanilla
1 6-ounce package (1 cup) semisweet
   chocolate pieces, melted and cooled

Combine first 2 ingredients; cut in butter or margarine till crumbly. Stir in chopped nuts; set aside. Sift together dry ingredients into large mixing bowl. Add shortening, eggs, buttermilk, and vanilla. Blend, then beat at medium speed on electric mixer 2 minutes.

Combine 1 cup batter and the melted, cooled chocolate. Alternate light and dark batters by spoonfuls in greased and lightly floured 13x9x2-inch baking pan; cut through to marble. Sprinkle with reserved crumbly nut mixture. Bake in moderate oven (350°) for about 30 minutes or till cake tests done. Cool.

# ELEGANT WHITE CAKES

## PETITS FOURS

Cream ¼ cup butter and ¼ cup shortening. Gradually add 1 cup sugar, creaming till light. Add ½ teaspoon vanilla and ¼ teaspoon almond extract. Sift together 2 cups sifted cake flour, 3 teaspoons baking powder, and ¼ teaspoon salt; add to creamed mixture alternately with ¾ cup milk. Beat well after each addition. Beat ¾ cup (6) egg whites till foamy; gradually add ¼ cup sugar and beat to soft peaks. Fold into batter. Bake in greased and lightly floured 13x9x2-inch pan at 350° about 40 minutes. Cool 10 minutes before removing from pan.

When cool, cut in 1½-inch diamonds or squares. Line up on rack with cookie sheet below. Spoon Icing evenly over cakes. (If too thick, add a few drops hot water.) Give cakes two coats of icing. Pipe frosting flower on each.

*Icing:* Cook 3 cups granulated sugar, ¼ teaspoon cream of tartar, and 1½ cups hot water to thin syrup (226°). Cool to lukewarm (110°). Add 1 teaspoon vanilla; add sifted confectioners' sugar (about 2½ cups) till icing is of consistency to pour. Tint with food coloring.

For smooth icing on Petits Fours, place cakes on rack over cookie sheet; pour icing evenly over cakes. Keep icing over hot water.

## MARASCHINO CHERRY CAKE

½ cup shortening
2¼ cups sifted cake flour
1⅛ cups sugar
3 teaspoons baking powder
½ teaspoon salt

• • •

¼ cup maraschino cherry juice
16 maraschino cherries, cut in eighths
½ cup milk
3 to 4 drops almond extract
4 unbeaten egg whites
½ cup chopped California walnuts

Place shortening in mixing bowl. Sift in dry ingredients. Add cherry juice, cherries, milk, and almond extract; mix till all flour is moistened. Beat vigorously 2 minutes. Add egg whites; beat vigorously 2 minutes longer. Fold in nuts. Bake in 2 greased and lightly floured 8x1½-inch round pans in moderate oven (350°) 30 to 35 minutes, or till cake tests done. Cool 10 minutes before removing from pans. Cool. Fill and frost with fluffy white frosting prepared from a mix.

Honor a bride or a "sweet sixteen" young lady with a pretty pink party. Serve iced Petits Fours and ice cream refreshments.

50

The most beautiful cake in any girl's life is her wedding cake. This cake, designed for a small reception, is made from three 13x9x 2-inch Petits Fours cakes, two stacked for the base, the third halved and stacked atop. Then it is frosted and decorated with Boiled Frosting and Sugar Bells (see Index).

Decoration on top of cake features a large sugar bell and a base molded from a gelatin mold. Heart frame is shaped from pipe cleaners trimmed with pleated tulle and beading, available at notions counters.

This white cake, baked in a heart-shaped pan, wears a nosegay of sugared flowers, one of the easiest cake decoration ideas.

Choose small flowers for sugaring such as tiny roses, carnations, and bachelor buttons. Beat 1 egg white slightly and stir in 1 tablespoon water. Brush egg white on petals with a small, soft brush. Sprinkle with sugar and place on cooling rack to dry. Store in dry place till used. To make nosegay, clip stems closely and insert in large dollop of frosting in center of doily. Place doily on cake.

## BUTTERMILK WHITE CAKE

2½ cups sifted cake flour
1½ cups sugar
1 teaspoon salt
1 teaspoon soda
1 teaspoon baking powder
¼ cup butter or margarine
¼ cup shortening
1½ teaspoons vanilla
1 cup buttermilk
4 egg whites

Sift together dry ingredients into large mixing bowl. Add butter, shortening, vanilla, and ¾ *cup* buttermilk; beat 2 minutes at medium speed on electric mixer. Add remaining buttermilk and egg whites; beat 2 minutes longer. Bake in 2 greased and lightly floured 8x1½-inch round pans in moderate oven (350°) 30 to 35 minutes. Cool. Frost with Seven Minute Frosting.

## POPPY-SEED CAKE

⅓ cup poppy seed
¾ cup milk
¾ cup butter or margarine
1½ cups sugar
1½ teaspoons vanilla
2 cups sifted cake flour
2½ teaspoons baking powder
¼ teaspoon salt
4 stiff-beaten egg whites
Cream Filling

Soak poppy seed in milk about 1 hour. Cream butter. Add sugar gradually, creaming till light and fluffy. Beat in vanilla, milk, and poppy seed. Sift together dry ingredients; stir into creamed mixture. Fold in egg whites. Bake in 2 greased and lightly floured 8x1½-inch round pans in moderate oven (375°) 20 to 25 minutes or till done. Cool 10 minutes before removing from pans. Cool thoroughly.

*Cream Filling.* Mix ½ cup sugar and 1 tablespoon cornstarch in saucepan. Combine 1½ cups milk and 4 slightly beaten egg yolks; gradually add to sugar mixture, stirring well. Cook and stir till mixture thickens and boils about 1 minute. Cool slightly. Add 1 teaspoon vanilla and ¼ cup chopped California walnuts.

Split cooled cake layers. Spread cooled filling between layers. Chill 2 to 3 hours before serving. Sift confectioners' sugar over top.

## WHITE CAKE SUPREME

*A perfect Valentine or birthday cake—*

¾ cup shortening
1½ cups sugar
1½ teaspoons vanilla
2¼ cups sifted cake flour
3 teaspoons baking powder
1 teaspoon salt
1 cup milk
5 stiff-beaten egg whites

Cream shortening and sugar till light and fluffy. Add vanilla; mix well. Sift together flour, baking powder, and salt. Add to creamed mixture alternately with milk, beginning and ending with dry ingredients and beating after each addition. Beat 2 minutes at medium speed on electric mixer. Fold in egg whites. Bake in 2 greased and lightly floured 9x1½-inch round pans in moderate oven (375°) for 18 to 20 minutes or till cake tests done. Cool 10 minutes before removing from pans. Fill and frost cooled layers with your favorite chocolate frosting.

## CREAMY WHITE CAKE

*For a variation, prepare a lemon pudding and pie filling mix for the filling of this cake—*

1 cup butter or margarine
1¾ cups sugar
6 egg whites
3 cups sifted cake flour
4 teaspoons baking powder
¾ teaspoon salt
¾ cup milk
½ cup water
1 teaspoon vanilla

Cream butter. Add sugar gradually, creaming till light and fluffy. Add the egg whites, two at a time, beating well after each addition. Sift together flour, baking powder, and salt. Combine milk, water, and vanilla. Add sifted dry ingredients to creamed mixture alternately with liquid, beginning and ending with dry ingredients. Beat smooth after each addition. Bake in 2 greased and lightly floured 9x1½-inch round pans in moderate oven (350°) for 30 to 35 minutes or till cake tests done. Fill and frost cooled layers with butter-type frosting.

# GOLDEN YELLOW CAKES

## BURNT-SUGAR CAKE

*A tender, tawny-golden cake with burnt-sugar flavor—*

½ cup shortening
1½ cups sugar
1 teaspoon vanilla
2 eggs
2½ cups sifted cake flour
3 teaspoons baking powder
½ teaspoon salt
¾ cup cold water
3 tablespoons Burnt-sugar Syrup*
Date Filling

Cream shortening and sugar till light. Add vanilla, then eggs, one at a time, beating 1 minute after each. Sift together dry ingredients and add to creamed mixture alternately with water, beating smooth after each addition. Add sugar syrup. Beat thoroughly, 4 minutes at medium speed on electric mixer.

Bake in 2 greased and lightly floured 9x1½-inch round cake pans at 375° about 20 minutes or till done. (Or bake in two 8x1½-inch round pans at 350° for 25 to 30 minutes.) Cool 10 minutes; remove from pans. Cool. Fill with Date Filling and frost with Burnt-sugar Frosting (see Index). Press broken walnuts on sides of cake.

*Date Filling:* Combine 1½ cups pitted dates, cut up, 1 cup water, ⅓ cup sugar, and ¼ teaspoon salt in saucepan; bring to boiling. Cook and stir over low heat about 4 minutes or till thick. Remove from heat; cool to room temperature. Fold in ¼ cup Burnt-sugar Frosting and ¼ cup chopped California walnuts.

*For Burnt-sugar Syrup, melt (caramelize) ⅔ cup granulated sugar in large heavy skillet, stirring constantly. When a deep golden brown syrup, remove from heat. Slowly add ⅔ cup boiling water. Heat and stir till all dissolves. Boil to reduce syrup to ½ cup. Cool. This is enough syrup for both cake and frosting.

**Yellow Cake Deluxe will leave no doubts about your mastery of cake baking. The smooth lemon filling, Seven Minute Frosting, and coconut are finishing touches.**

## YELLOW CAKE DELUXE

⅔ cup butter or margarine
1¾ cups sugar
2 eggs
1½ teaspoons vanilla
3 cups sifted cake flour
2½ teaspoons baking powder
1 teaspoon salt
1¼ cups milk
Lemon Filling

Cream butter. Add sugar gradually, creaming till light. Add eggs and vanilla and beat till fluffy. Sift dry ingredients together; add to creamed mixture alternately with milk, beating after each addition. Beat 1 minute. Bake in 2 greased and lightly floured 9x1½-inch round pans at 350° for 30 to 35 minutes. Cool 10 minutes; remove from pans. Cool. Fill with Lemon Filling; frost with Seven Minute Frosting.

*Lemon Filling:* Combine ¾ cup sugar, 2 tablespoons cornstarch, and dash salt in a saucepan. Add ¾ cup water, 2 slightly beaten egg yolks, and 3 tablespoons lemon juice; cook over medium heat till thick, stirring constantly. Remove from heat; add 1 teaspoon grated lemon peel and 1 tablespoon butter or margarine. Cool.

## LOAF POUND CAKE

¾ cup butter or margarine
¾ cup sugar
1 teaspoon vanilla
½ teaspoon grated lemon peel
3 eggs
1¼ cups sifted all-purpose flour
½ teaspoon baking powder
¼ teaspoon salt

Cream butter; gradually add sugar, creaming till light, about 6 minutes. Beat in vanilla and peel. Add eggs, one at a time, beating well after each. Sift together dry ingredients. Stir in. Grease bottom only of 9x5x3-inch pan; turn in batter. Bake at 350° for 50 minutes or till done. Cool in pan. Dust with confectioners' sugar.

## TOASTED BUTTER PECAN CAKE

3 tablespoons butter or margarine
1⅓ cups chopped pecans
¾ cup butter or margarine
1⅓ cups sugar
1½ teaspoons vanilla
2 eggs
2 cups sifted all-purpose flour
2 teaspoons baking powder
¼ teaspoon salt
⅔ cup milk
Butter Pecan Frosting

Dot 3 tablespoons butter over chopped pecans in shallow pan. Toast in moderate oven (350°) 15 minutes, stirring occasionally.

Cream ¾ cup butter; add sugar gradually, creaming till light. Add vanilla. Add eggs, one at a time, beating well after each. Sift together dry ingredients and add to creamed mixture alternately with milk, beating after each addition. Fold in *1 cup* of the toasted pecans. Bake in 2 greased and lightly floured 8x1½-inch round pans in moderate oven (350°) for 30 to 35 minutes, or till cake tests done. Cool 10 minutes; remove from pans. Cool completely.

Frost with *Butter Pecan Frosting:* Mix till smooth 4 tablespoons butter or margarine, softened, 3 cups sifted confectioners' sugar, 2½ to 3 tablespoons light cream, and 1 teaspoon vanilla. Stir in remaining toasted pecans.

## BANANA CAKE WITH CREAMY STRAWBERRY FLUFF

Place ⅔ cup shortening in mixing bowl. Sift in 2½ cups sifted cake flour, 1⅔ cups sugar, 1¼ teaspoons baking powder, 1 teaspoon soda, and 1 teaspoon salt. Add 1¼ cups mashed fully ripe bananas and ⅓ cup buttermilk *or* sour milk; mix till moistened. Beat vigorously 2 minutes. Add ⅓ cup buttermilk *or* sour milk and 2 eggs; beat 2 minutes longer. Bake in 2 greased and lightly floured 8x1½-inch round pans in moderate oven (350°) about 40 minutes or till done. Cool 10 minutes; remove from pans. Cool.

Fill and frost with *Creamy Strawberry Fluff:* In large mixing bowl, whip 2 cups whipping cream till thick but not stiff. Add 1 cup vanilla ice cream by spoonfuls, beating just till smooth. Fold in 2 cups sliced fresh strawberries. Garnish frosted cake with sugar-coated strawberries.

## CARROT-PINEAPPLE CAKE

*A moist, flavorful cake with a delicious, rich frosting—*

Sift together into large mixing bowl 1½ cups sifted all-purpose flour, 1 cup sugar, 1 teaspoon baking powder, 1 teaspoon soda, 1 teaspoon cinnamon, and ½ teaspoon salt. Add ⅔ cup salad oil, 2 eggs, 1 cup finely shredded carrot, ½ cup crushed pineapple (with syrup), and 1 teaspoon vanilla. Mix till all ingredients are moistened; beat 2 minutes at medium speed on electric mixer. Bake in greased and lightly floured 9x9x2-inch pan in moderate oven (350°) about 35 minutes or till done. Cool.

Frost with *Cream Cheese Frosting:* Cream together one 3-ounce package cream cheese and 4 tablespoons butter or margarine; beat in 1 teaspoon vanilla and dash salt. Gradually add 2½ cups sifted confectioners' sugar, blending well. Stir in ½ cup chopped pecans.

## ORANGE CELEBRATION CAKE

*Doubly orange with fresh juice in both cake and filling—*

⅓ cup butter or margarine
⅓ cup shortening
2 teaspoons grated orange peel
1½ cups sugar
3 eggs
2½ cups sifted cake flour
2½ teaspoons baking powder
1 teaspoon salt
1 cup orange juice
Orange Filling

Cream together butter, shortening, and peel. Gradually add sugar, creaming till light. Add eggs, one at a time, beating well after each. Sift together dry ingredients and add alternately with orange juice to creamed mixture, beating after each addition. Bake in 2 greased and lightly floured 9x1½-inch round pans in moderate oven (350°) 25 to 30 minutes or till done. Cool 10 minutes; remove from pans. Cool.

Fill layers with *Orange Filling:* Combine ⅔ cup sugar and 3 tablespoons all-purpose flour in saucepan. Add 1 cup orange juice and 2 egg yolks. Cook and stir till mixture boils; cook 1 minute. Stir in 2 tablespoons butter; cool.

Frost cake with Seven Minute Frosting. If desired, sprinkle top and sides with flaked coconut.

Gingerbread, warm, spicy, and fragrant, brings back memories of happy days in Grandma's kitchen. But gingerbread suits modern tastes, too, with a fluffy citrus topper.

# SAVORY SPICE CAKES

## GINGERBREAD

Gradually add ½ cup sugar to ½ cup shortening, creaming till light. Add 1 egg and ½ cup light molasses; beat thoroughly. Sift together 1½ cups sifted all-purpose flour, ¾ teaspoon salt, ¾ teaspoon soda, ½ teaspoon ginger, and ½ teaspoon cinnamon. Add to creamed mixture alternately with ½ cup boiling water, beating after each addition. Bake in well-greased 8x8x2-inch pan in moderate oven (350°) 35 to 40 minutes or till done. Serve warm with Citrus Fluff.

*Citrus Fluff:* In small saucepan, beat 1 egg; add ½ cup sugar, 1 teaspoon grated orange peel, 1 teaspoon grated lemon peel, and 2 tablespoons lemon juice. Cook and stir over low heat till thick, about 5 minutes. Cool thoroughly. Fold in 1 cup whipping cream, whipped. Chill. Spoon onto squares of warm gingerbread. Garnish with a twist of orange. Makes about 2 cups topping.

## MOLASSES POUND CAKE

½ cup shortening
½ cup sugar
2 eggs
½ cup molasses
2 cups sifted cake flour
2 teaspoons baking powder
1 teaspoon cinnamon
½ teaspoon salt
½ teaspoon nutmeg
¼ teaspoon cloves
⅔ cup milk

Cream shortening and sugar together. Add eggs; beat well. Stir in molasses. Sift together dry ingredients; add alternately with milk to creamed mixture. Bake in well-greased and lightly floured 6-cup Bundt mold at 350° about 40 minutes. Cool 1 hour; remove from pan.

## HARVEST APPLE CAKE

2 cups sifted all-purpose flour
1 cup granulated sugar
1½ teaspoons soda
1 teaspoon salt
1 teaspoon cinnamon
¼ teaspoon nutmeg
¼ cup brown sugar
½ cup shortening
1 cup apple juice
1½ cups finely chopped pared apples
2 eggs
½ cup raisins
½ cup chopped California walnuts
Apple Frosting

Sift together first 6 ingredients into mixing bowl. Stir in brown sugar. Add shortening, apple juice, and chopped apple; beat till smooth, about 2 minutes at medium speed on electric mixer. Add eggs; beat well. Stir in raisins and nuts. Bake in greased 13x9x2-inch pan in moderate oven (350°) 30 to 35 minutes or till cake tests done. Cool; frost with Apple Frosting.

*Apple Frosting:* Beat together 2 tablespoons butter or margarine, 1 cup sifted confectioners' sugar, and ½ teaspoon vanilla. Add 1 to 2 tablespoons apple juice, beating till frosting is of spreading consistency.

## APPLESAUCE CAKE

2½ cups sifted all-purpose flour
2 cups sugar
1½ teaspoons soda
1½ teaspoons salt
¾ teaspoon cinnamon
½ teaspoon allspice
½ teaspoon cloves
½ cup shortening
½ cup water
1½ cups applesauce
1 egg
½ cup chopped California walnuts
½ cup golden raisins

Sift dry ingredients into large mixing bowl. Add shortening and water; beat 1 minute with electric mixer. Add applesauce and egg; beat 3 minutes. Stir in nuts and raisins. Pour into a greased and floured 13x9x2-inch baking pan. Bake at 350° for 35 to 40 minutes. Cool; frost.

## CARAMEL GINGER CAKE

Cream ½ cup butter or margarine. Gradually add 1½ cups brown sugar, creaming well. Add 1 teaspoon vanilla. Add 2 eggs, one at a time, beating well after each. Sift 2½ cups sifted all-purpose flour with 2 teaspoons baking powder, 1 teaspoon salt, 1 teaspoon ground ginger, and ¼ teaspoon soda; add to creamed mixture alternately with 1½ cups milk, beating well after each addition. Bake in greased and lightly floured 13x9x2-inch baking pan in moderate oven (350°) for 35 to 40 minutes or till done. Cool thoroughly. Frost with Tutti-frutti Frosting.

*Tutti-frutti Frosting:* In top of double boiler, combine 1 egg white, ¾ cup sugar, 1 teaspoon light corn syrup, 3 tablespoons cold water, and dash salt. Beat 1 minute with electric or rotary beater to blend. Place over boiling water and cook, beating constantly, till stiff peaks form, about 4 minutes. Remove from water; add ½ teaspoon vanilla and 3 drops almond extract; beat to spreading consistency. Fold in ½ cup *each* golden raisins and chopped California walnuts, and 1 tablespoon chopped candied ginger.

## NUTMEG CAKE

½ cup butter or margarine
1⅓ cups granulated sugar
3 eggs
2 cups sifted all-purpose flour
1 teaspoon baking powder
1 teaspoon soda
1½ to 2 teaspoons nutmeg
½ teaspoon salt
1 cup buttermilk *or* sour milk
6 tablespoons butter or margarine
¼ cup light cream
1 cup brown sugar
½ cup flaked coconut

Cream butter. Add sugar gradually, creaming till fluffy. Add eggs, one at a time, beating well after each. Sift together dry ingredients and add alternately with buttermilk, beating till smooth after each addition. Bake in greased and lightly floured 13x9x2-inch baking pan in moderate oven (375°) for 20 minutes or till done.

*Topping:* Bring butter, light cream, and brown sugar to boiling. Remove cake from oven; pour hot mixture slowly over cake; sprinkle with coconut. Return to oven; bake 5 minutes longer.

## SPICE NUT CAKE

2 cups sifted all-purpose flour
1 cup granulated sugar
1 teaspoon baking powder
1 teaspoon salt
¾ teaspoon soda
¾ teaspoon cloves
¾ teaspoon cinnamon

• • •

⅔ cup shortening
¾ cup brown sugar
1 cup buttermilk *or* sour milk
3 eggs
½ cup finely chopped California walnuts

Sift flour, granulated sugar, baking powder, salt, soda, and spices into large mixing bowl. Add shortening, brown sugar, and buttermilk. Mix till all flour is moistened. Beat with electric or rotary beater 2 minutes. Add eggs; beat 2 minutes more. Stir in nuts. Bake in 2 greased and lightly floured 9x1½-inch round cake pans in moderate oven (350°) for 30 to 35 minutes, or till cake tests done. Cool 10 minutes before removing from pans. Cool thoroughly. Fill and frost with Orange Butter Frosting.

## MOLASSES MINT CAKE

¾ cup shortening
2 cups sifted all-purpose flour
⅔ cup sugar
1 teaspoon soda
¾ teaspoon salt
1 teaspoon cinnamon

• • •

3 eggs
⅔ cup molasses
½ cup milk
½ cup broken solid chocolate-mint
   candy wafers

Place shortening in mixing bowl. Sift together flour, sugar, soda, salt, and cinnamon. Add to shortening. Add *2 eggs* and molasses; beat 2 minutes at medium speed on electric mixer. Add remaining egg and milk and beat 2 minutes longer. Pour into 2 greased and lightly floured 9x1½-inch round pans. Sprinkle candy over batter. Bake at 350° for 25 to 30 minutes or till done. Cool 10 minutes. Remove from pans; cool. Frost with fluffy white frosting.

## PUMPKIN SPICE CAKE

Cream ½ cup shortening and 1⅓ cups sugar till fluffy. Add 2 eggs, one at a time, beating well after each. Combine 1 cup canned pumpkin and ⅔ cup buttermilk *or* sour milk. Sift together 1¾ cups sifted all-purpose flour, 2 teaspoons baking powder, 1 teaspoon soda, 1 teaspoon salt, 2 teaspoons cinnamon, ½ teaspoon nutmeg, ¼ teaspoon allspice, and ¼ teaspoon ginger. Add to creamed mixture alternately with pumpkin mixture, beating well after each addition. Bake in greased and lightly floured 13x9x2-inch pan at 350° for 40 to 45 minutes. Cool; frost with Golden Butter Frosting.

## SESAME CAKE

2¼ cups sifted cake flour
1½ cups sugar
3 teaspoons baking powder
½ teaspoon salt
¼ teaspoon mace
½ cup toasted sesame seed*
½ cup shortening
1¼ cups milk
2 eggs

Sift together dry ingredients; stir in seed. Add shortening and ¾ *cup* milk. Beat 2 minutes on electric mixer. Add remaining milk and eggs; beat 1 minute. Pour into 2 greased and floured 8x1½-inch round pans. Bake at 350° for about 25 minutes. Frost with Sea Foam Frosting.

*To toast seed, spread in shallow pan; heat in 350° oven for 10 minutes; stir occasionally.

## FEATHERY CRUMB CAKE

Combine 1 cup butter or margarine, 1 cup granulated sugar, 1 cup brown sugar, and 3 cups sifted all-purpose flour; reserve 1 cup for crumb topping. To remaining mixture, add 2 eggs; beat till light. Sift together ½ cup sifted all-purpose flour, 1 teaspoon baking powder, 1 teaspoon soda, 1 teaspoon cinnamon, ½ teaspoon cloves, ½ teaspoon allspice, ½ teaspoon nutmeg, and ¼ teaspoon salt. Add alternately with 1 cup sour milk *or* buttermilk, beating till smooth. Pour into greased and lightly floured 13x9x2-inch baking pan. Sprinkle with reserved crumb topping. Bake at 350° for 45 minutes or till done.

# CUPCAKE TREATS

## CRANBERRY CUPCAKES

½ cup shortening
1 cup brown sugar
2 eggs
1½ cups sifted all-purpose flour
1 teaspoon cinnamon
1 teaspoon nutmeg
½ teaspoon salt
½ teaspoon soda
½ cup dairy sour cream
½ cup canned jellied cranberry sauce
½ cup chopped California walnuts

Cream shortening and sugar together thoroughly. Add eggs and beat well. Sift together dry ingredients and add to creamed mixture alternately with sour cream and cranberry sauce, beating till smooth. Stir in nuts. Fill paper bake cups in muffin pans half full. Bake at 350° for 20 to 25 minutes. Cool. Frost with Golden Butter Frosting and trim with cutouts of jellied cranberry sauce. Makes about 2 dozen cupcakes.

## APPLE-ORANGE CUPCAKES

6 tablespoons butter or margarine
1 cup brown sugar
½ cup applesauce
1 teaspoon shredded orange peel
1 teaspoon vanilla
1 egg
1 cup sifted all-purpose flour
1 teaspoon baking powder
½ teaspoon salt
¼ teaspoon soda
½ cup chopped California walnuts

Combine butter and sugar in saucepan. Heat and stir till butter melts. Beat in applesauce, orange peel, vanilla, and egg. Sift together dry ingredients; stir into applesauce mixture. Stir in nuts. Fill paper bake cups in muffin pans half full. Bake at 350° for 20 to 25 minutes. Cool. Frost with Orange Butter Frosting. Makes 12.

Perky jellied cranberry sauce topknots spicy Cranberry Cupcakes. Baked in the batter, cranberry gives the spicy flavor extra punch.

## MOCHA CUPCAKES

½ cup shortening
1 cup sugar
1 egg
1 teaspoon vanilla
1⅓ cups sifted all-purpose flour
1 teaspoon baking powder
½ teaspoon soda
¼ teaspoon salt
½ cup cocoa (regular-type, dry)
½ cup milk
1½ teaspoons instant coffee powder

Cream shortening and sugar well. Add egg and vanilla; beat well. Beat in sifted dry ingredients alternately with milk. Dissolve coffee in ½ cup hot water; stir into batter. Fill paper bake cups in muffin pans ⅔ full. Bake at 375° for 20 minutes. Cool and frost. Makes about 18 cupcakes.

## YELLOW CUPCAKES

⅓ cup shortening
1¾ cups sifted cake flour
¾ cup sugar
2½ teaspoons baking powder
½ teaspoon salt
1 egg
¾ cup milk
½ teaspoon vanilla

Place shortening in mixing bowl; sift in dry ingredients. Add egg and ½ cup milk; mix till flour is moistened. Beat 2 minutes at medium speed on electric mixer. Add ¼ cup milk and vanilla; beat 2 minutes longer. Fill paper bake cups in muffin pans half full. Bake at 375° for 20 to 25 minutes. Cool. Frost with Golden Butter Frosting. Makes about 18 cupcakes.

For *Pink-peppermint Cupcakes:* Prepare Yellow Cupcakes; add ½ teaspoon peppermint extract and a few drops red food coloring with vanilla. Stir 2 tablespoons crushed peppermint-stick candy into Golden Butter Frosting. Frost cupcakes. Sprinkle tops with crushed candy.

For *Lemon Cupcakes:* Prepare Yellow Cupcakes; add ½ teaspoon grated lemon peel. Frost with Seven Minute Frosting. Top with coconut.

# UPSIDE-DOWN AND PUDDING CAKES

## PINEAPPLE UPSIDE-DOWN CAKE

2 tablespoons butter or margarine
½ cup brown sugar
1 14½-ounce can sliced pineapple
   (4 slices)
4 maraschino cherries, halved
⅓ cup shortening
1¼ cups sifted all-purpose flour
½ cup granulated sugar
2 teaspoons baking powder
½ teaspoon salt
½ teaspoon grated lemon peel
1 egg

Melt butter in an 8x8x2-inch pan. Stir in brown sugar. Drain pineapple, reserving ½ cup syrup; cut slices in half. Arrange atop sugar, placing a cherry half in each hollow.

Place shortening in mixing bowl. Add sifted dry ingredients. Add remaining ingredients and reserved pineapple syrup; mix till flour is moistened. Beat vigorously 2 minutes. Pour over pineapple. Bake at 350° for 30 to 35 minutes or till done. Cool 10 minutes; invert on plate. Serve warm with whipped cream.

## COCONUT-APRICOT CAKE

*A "company best" upside-down cake—*

Melt 6 tablespoons butter or margarine in an 8x8x2-inch baking pan. Stir in ⅔ cup brown sugar, 1 tablespoon light corn syrup, and one 3½-ounce can (1⅓ cups) flaked coconut. Pat evenly on bottom and sides of pan. Arrange one 1-pound can apricot halves, drained, cut side up, over coconut in bottom of pan.

Into small mixing bowl, sift 1 cup sifted all-purpose flour, ¾ cup granulated sugar, 1¼ teaspoons baking powder, and ¼ teaspoon salt. Add ¼ cup shortening, 1 egg, ½ cup milk, and ½ teaspoon vanilla; blend at low speed on electric mixer, then beat at medium speed 2 minutes. Spread over apricots. Bake in a moderate oven (375°) for 45 to 50 minutes. Cool 1 to 2 minutes; turn out on plate. Serve warm.

## RHUBARB UPSIDE-DOWN CAKE

2 tablespoons butter or margarine
½ cup granulated sugar
¼ cup brown sugar
2 cups rhubarb cut in ½-inch pieces
⅓ cup shortening
½ cup granulated sugar
1 egg
½ teaspoon vanilla
1 cup sifted all-purpose flour
1½ teaspoons baking powder
¼ teaspoon salt
½ cup milk

Melt butter in 8x8x2-inch baking pan; stir in ½ cup granulated sugar, brown sugar, and rhubarb. Spread evenly over bottom of pan. In small mixing bowl, cream shortening and ½ cup sugar; add egg and vanilla; beat well. Sift together dry ingredients. Add alternately with milk to creamed mixture. Spread over rhubarb. Bake at 350° for 50 to 55 minutes. Cool 10 minutes before inverting on serving plate. Serve warm with whipped cream.

## PEACH PUDDING CAKE

2 cups sifted all-purpose flour
2 tablespoons granulated sugar
½ teaspoon salt
¼ teaspoon baking powder
½ cup butter or margarine
10 peach halves, fresh or canned
1 cup light brown sugar
1 teaspoon cinnamon
2 slightly beaten egg yolks
1 cup whipping cream

Sift first 4 ingredients together. Cut in butter till mixture resembles cornmeal; sprinkle over bottom and sides of greased 8¼x1¾-inch round ovenware cake dish. Place peaches, cut side up, over crumb mixture. Combine brown sugar and cinnamon; sprinkle over peaches. Bake at 400° for 15 minutes. Combine egg yolks and cream; pour over peaches; bake 30 to 35 minutes or till knife inserted comes out clean. Serve warm.

Rich, tender Date Pudding Cake sauces itself. Best of all, it's mixed, baked, and served in the same dish. A real work-saver.

## DATE PUDDING CAKE

Snip 1 cup pitted dates into a 9-inch round or square baking dish; add 2 tablespoons butter or margarine. Pour 1 cup boiling water over; stir to melt butter and soften dates. Add 1 egg, 1½ cups instant-type flour, ½ cup granulated sugar, ½ cup brown sugar, 1 teaspoon soda, ½ teaspoon baking powder, ½ teaspoon salt, and ½ cup broken California walnuts.

Beat with fork till mixture is thoroughly blended, about 2 minutes. Scrape bottom and sides of baking dish with rubber spatula after 1 minute of beating.

Smooth batter evenly in baking dish; sprinkle with 1½ cups brown sugar. Slowly pour 1½ cups boiling water over all. Bake in moderate oven (375°) about 40 minutes or till cake tests done. Serve warm with scoops of vanilla ice cream piled in center of cake.

## FUDGE PUDDING CAKE

*Chocolate fans, take note of this double fudge treat—*

1½ cups sifted all-purpose flour
¾ cup granulated sugar
½ teaspoon soda
½ teaspoon salt
1 1-ounce square unsweetened chocolate
2 tablespoons butter or margarine
¾ cup sour milk
½ teaspoon vanilla
¾ cup coarsely chopped California walnuts

• • •

¾ cup brown sugar
1½ cups boiling water
2 1-ounce squares unsweetened chocolate

Sift flour, granulated sugar, soda, and salt together. Melt 1 square chocolate with butter. Stir in sour milk and vanilla. Add to dry ingredients; stir till blended. Mix in walnuts. Turn into a greased 8x8x2-inch baking pan.

Sprinkle brown sugar over top. Combine boiling water and 2 squares chocolate; stir till chocolate melts. Pour evenly over sugar topping. Bake in moderate oven (350°) 40 to 45 minutes or till cake is done. Serve warm.

## LEMON PUDDING CAKE

*Just the right dessert to top off a meal. Airy light cake tops delicately flavored lemon pudding—*

¾ cup sugar
Dash salt
3 tablespoons butter or margarine, melted
¼ cup sifted all-purpose flour
1 teaspoon grated lemon peel
¼ cup lemon juice

• • •

1½ cups milk
3 well beaten egg yolks
3 stiff-beaten egg whites

Combine sugar, salt, and butter. Stir in flour, then lemon peel and juice. Combine milk and egg yolks; add to lemon mixture. Fold in egg whites. Pour into 8x8x2-inch baking pan and place in pan of hot water. Bake in moderate oven (350°) 40 minutes or till top is lightly browned. Serve warm or chilled.

# THE LIGHTEST CAKES EVER

## ANGEL CAKE

1 cup sifted cake flour
¾ cup sugar
12 egg whites (1½ cups)
1½ teaspoons cream of tartar
¼ teaspoon salt
1½ teaspoons vanilla
¾ cup sugar

Sift flour with ¾ cup sugar 4 times; set aside. Beat egg whites with cream of tartar, salt, and vanilla till stiff enough to form soft peaks but still moist and glossy. Add remaining ¾ cup sugar, 2 tablespoons at a time, continuing to beat till egg whites hold stiff peaks. Sift about ¼ of flour mixture over whites; fold in. Repeat, folding in remaining flour by fourths. Bake in *ungreased* 10-inch tube pan in moderate oven (375°) 35 to 40 minutes, or till done. Invert cake in pan; cool. Remove from pan.

For **Raspberry Angel Dessert:** Slice cake in 3 layers. Make *Custard-whipped Cream Filling:* In saucepan, mix ½ cup sugar, ⅓ cup all-purpose flour, and ½ teaspoon salt; slowly add 2 cups milk; mix well. Cook and stir over medium heat till mixture thickens and boils; cook 2 minutes more. Stir small amount of hot mixture into 3 slightly beaten egg yolks; return to hot mixture. Stirring constantly, bring just to boiling. Remove from heat; stir in 1 teaspoon vanilla. Cool. Fold in 1 cup whipping cream, whipped.

Reassemble cake, spreading filling between layers and on top. Garnish with frozen raspberries, slightly thawed, or sweetened fresh berries.

## CHOCOLATE ANGEL CAKE

Prepare Angel Cake, substituting ¾ cup sifted cake flour and ¼ cup cocoa (regular-type, dry) for 1 cup sifted cake flour. Sift cocoa together with flour and sugar 4 times.

Here's heavenly high Raspberry Angel Dessert crowned with raspberries and mint. Another time give this angel cake a new look with mandarin oranges or sliced peaches.

## MARBLE CHIFFON CAKE

2¼ cups sifted cake flour
1½ cups sugar
3 teaspoons baking powder
1 teaspoon salt
½ cup salad oil
7 egg yolks
¾ cup cold water
1 teaspoon vanilla
7 egg whites
½ teaspoon cream of tartar

• • •

¼ cup boiling water
2 tablespoons sugar
2 1-ounce squares unsweetened chocolate, melted

Sift together first 4 ingredients. Make well in center of dry ingredients and add in order next 4 ingredients. Beat till satin smooth. In large bowl, beat egg whites with cream of tartar till *very stiff peaks* form. Pour egg yolk mixture in thin stream over entire surface of egg whites, gently folding to blend. Remove ⅓ of batter to separate bowl. Blend last 3 ingredients; gently fold into ⅓ portion of batter. Spoon *half* the light batter into *ungreased* 10-inch tube pan; top with *half* the chocolate batter. Repeat layers. With narrow spatula, swirl gently through batters to marble. Bake in slow oven (325°) about 55 minutes or till cake tests done. Invert cake in pan; cool. Frost with chocolate frosting.

## BROWN SUGAR ANGEL CAKE

Beat 1½ cups (12) egg whites with 1½ teaspoons cream of tartar, 1 teaspoon salt, and 2 teaspoons vanilla till stiff enough to form soft peaks but still moist and glossy. Gradually *sieve* 1 cup brown sugar over egg whites and beat till stiff peaks form. Sift 1 cup brown sugar with 1¼ cups sifted cake flour; fold into egg whites. Bake in *ungreased* 10-inch tube pan in moderate oven (350°) 45 to 50 minutes, or till done. Invert cake in pan; cool. Frost with Fluffy White Frosting or whipped cream.

Lincoln Log is jelly roll deluxe! Not a speedy recipe, but it is easier to make than it looks and well worth the fuss. Filling for rich chocolate sponge cake is whipped cream.

## LINCOLN LOG

Sift together twice ½ cup sugar, ¼ cup sifted all-purpose flour, 3 tablespoons cocoa (regular-type, dry), and ¼ teaspoon salt. Beat 5 egg whites with ½ teaspoon cream of tartar till stiff but not dry; gradually add ½ cup sugar, beating constantly. Beat 5 egg yolks till thick and lemon-colored; add 1 teaspoon vanilla; fold in dry ingredients. Fold yolk batter into whites.

Spread batter evenly in greased and floured 15½x10½x1-inch pan. Bake at 325° about 25 minutes. Immediately turn cake out onto towel sprinkled with confectioners' sugar. Roll cake along with towel; cool. Unroll; spread 1 cup whipping cream, whipped, over cake; roll again. Spread with hot Chocolate Gloss; garnish with toasted sliced almonds. Chill. Serves 8 to 10.

*Chocolate Gloss:* Mix ½ cup sugar and 1½ tablespoons cornstarch; add one 1-ounce square unsweetened chocolate, dash salt, and ½ cup water. Cook and stir till thickened. Remove from heat; add 1½ tablespoons butter and ½ teaspoon vanilla. While hot, spread over rolled cake.

## TROPICAL CHIFFON CAKE

2¼ cups sifted cake flour
1½ cups sugar
3 teaspoons baking powder
1 teaspoon salt
½ cup salad oil
¾ cup (8) egg yolks
1 teaspoon grated orange peel *or*
  2 teaspoons grated lemon peel
¾ cup orange juice
1 cup (8) egg whites
½ teaspoon cream of tartar
1⅓ cups flaked coconut

Sift together dry ingredients into bowl. Make well in center; add in order next 4 ingredients; beat till satin smooth. Beat egg whites with cream of tartar to *very stiff peaks*. Pour batter in thin stream evenly over entire surface of egg whites; fold in gently. Fold in coconut. Bake in *ungreased* 10-inch tube pan at 325° about 55 minutes. Invert pan; cool. Frost with a butter frosting or yellow-tinted whipped cream.

# BOSTON CREAM PIE

1 cup sifted all-purpose flour
1 teaspoon baking powder
¼ teaspoon salt
2 tablespoons butter or margarine
½ cup *hot* milk
2 eggs
1 cup sugar
1 teaspoon vanilla

Sift together first 3 ingredients. Add butter to hot milk; *keep hot*. Beat eggs till thick and lemon-colored, about 3 minutes at high speed on electric mixer. Gradually add sugar, beating constantly at medium speed for about 5 minutes. Add vanilla; add sifted dry ingredients to egg mixture; stir just till blended. Stir in hot milk mixture; blend well. Bake in 2 greased and floured 8x1½-inch round pans at 350° for 25 to 30 minutes. Cool 10 minutes; remove from pans.

Prepare *Cream-custard Filling:* Combine in saucepan ⅓ cup sugar, 2 tablespoons flour, 1 tablespoon cornstarch, and ¼ teaspoon salt. Gradually add 1½ cups milk; mix well. Cook and stir over medium heat till mixture thickens and boils; cook and stir 2 to 3 minutes longer. Beat 1 egg with 1 egg yolk; stir a little hot mixture into eggs; return to hot mixture. Cook and stir till mixture just boils. Add 1 teaspoon vanilla. Cool. Spread over 1 cake layer, top with second layer.

Prepare *Chocolate Glaze:* Place one 1-ounce square unsweetened chocolate and 1 tablespoon butter in small saucepan. Stir over low heat till melted. Remove from heat; add 1 cup sifted confectioners' sugar and ½ teaspoon vanilla. Blend in enough boiling water to make of drizzling consistency. Spoon over cake.

# ORANGE SUNSHINE CAKE

Beat ¾ cup (8) egg yolks till thick and lemon-colored; gradually add ⅔ cup sugar, beating till thick. Combine 1 teaspoon grated orange peel and ½ cup orange juice; add alternately to egg mixture with 1 cup sifted cake flour.

Beat 1 cup (8) egg whites with 1 teaspoon cream of tartar and ½ teaspoon salt till soft peaks form; gradually add ⅔ cup sugar; beat till stiff peaks form. Fold into egg yolk mixture. Bake in *ungreased* 10-inch tube pan at 325° for about 1 hour and 10 to 15 minutes. Invert; cool.

# GOLDEN BUTTER SPONGE CAKE

In mixing bowl, cream 1 cup butter or margarine, softened, with 1 cup sugar till very light and fluffy. Add 6 egg yolks, one at a time, beating well after each addition. Beat till mixture is very fluffy and smooth, about 5 minutes. Sift together 2 cups sifted cake flour, ½ teaspoon baking powder, and ½ teaspoon salt; stir into butter mixture. Beat 6 egg whites till soft peaks form; gradually add ¾ cup sugar, beating till very stiff peaks form. Fold into butter mixture. Lightly grease bottom of 10-inch tube pan; pour in batter. Bake in moderate oven (350°) about 55 minutes or till done. Invert to cool.

# SNOW-CAPPED LEMON ROLL

4 egg yolks
⅔ cup sugar
½ teaspoon grated lemon peel
1 tablespoon lemon juice
4 egg whites
⅔ cup sifted cake flour
¼ teaspoon salt
Lemon Filling
Meringue

Beat the egg yolks till thick and lemon-colored. Gradually add ⅓ *cup* sugar, beating constantly. Stir in lemon peel and juice. Beat egg whites till soft peaks form; gradually add remaining ⅓ cup sugar and beat till stiff peaks form. Gently fold yolks into whites. Sift together flour and salt; fold into egg mixture. Spread batter evenly in greased and floured 15½x10½x1-inch pan. Bake at 350° about 15 minutes. Immediately turn out on towel sprinkled with confectioners' sugar. Starting at narrow end, roll cake and towel together; cool.

Prepare Lemon Filling. Unroll cake; spread with filling. Roll again. For Meringue: Beat 2 egg whites till soft peaks form. Gradually add ¼ cup sugar, beating till stiff peaks form. Spread meringue over top and sides of cake roll. Bake at 350° for 12 to 15 minutes. Makes 10 servings.

*Lemon Filling:* In saucepan, mix ¾ cup sugar and 2 tablespoons cornstarch. Gradually add ¾ cup water. Stir in 2 slightly beaten egg yolks and ¼ cup lemon juice. Cook and stir over medium heat till thick. Remove from heat; stir in 1 teaspoon grated lemon peel and 2 tablespoons butter or margarine. Cool to room temperature.

# LUSCIOUS TORTES

## PUMPKIN DATE TORTE

Mix ½ cup chopped dates, ½ cup chopped California walnuts, and 2 tablespoons all-purpose flour; set aside. Melt ¼ cup butter or margarine over low heat; blend in 1 cup brown sugar. Remove from heat; stir in ⅔ cup canned pumpkin and 1 teaspoon vanilla. Beat in 2 eggs, one at a time. Sift together ½ cup sifted all-purpose flour, ½ teaspoon baking powder, ½ teaspoon cinnamon, ½ teaspoon nutmeg, ¼ teaspoon soda, and ¼ teaspoon ginger; add to pumpkin mixture; mix well. Stir in floured dates and nuts. Bake in greased 9x1½-inch round pan in a moderate oven (350°) for 20 to 25 minutes. Serve warm with whipped cream.

## BUTTERSCOTCH TORTE

6 egg yolks
1½ cups granulated sugar
1 teaspoon baking powder
2 teaspoons vanilla
1 teaspoon almond extract
6 egg whites
2 cups graham-cracker crumbs
1 cup chopped pecans

• • • •

1 cup whipping cream, whipped
½ teaspoon vanilla
1 cup brown sugar
¼ cup butter or margarine
¼ cup orange juice
¼ cup water
2 eggs, slightly beaten
½ teaspoon vanilla

Beat egg yolks till thick and lemon-colored. Gradually add sugar and baking powder, beating well. Add flavorings. Beat egg whites till stiff peaks form. Gradually fold in egg yolks, cracker crumbs, and nuts. Bake in 9-inch spring-form pan at 325° for 50 to 55 minutes. Cool. To whipped cream, add ½ teaspoon vanilla. Spoon atop torte. Trim center with chopped walnuts. Make wreath of walnut halves around edge. Cut in wedges. Serve with Brown Sugar Sauce.

*Brown Sugar Sauce:* Combine brown sugar, butter, orange juice, water, and eggs. Cook and stir till mixture thickens. Add vanilla; chill.

## KONA COFFEE TORTE

Dissolve 1½ tablespoons instant coffee powder in 1 cup cold water. Beat 6 egg yolks till light; gradually add 2 cups sugar, beating till thick. Sift together 2 cups sifted all-purpose flour, 3 teaspoons baking powder, and ¼ teaspoon salt; add to egg yolks alternately with coffee, beating after each addition. Add 1 teaspoon vanilla and 1 cup ground California walnuts. Fold in 6 stiff-beaten egg whites.

Bake in 3 paper-lined 9x1½-inch round pans in slow oven (325°) 30 minutes or till done. Fill cooled cake with Orange Filling, frost with Mocha Frosting. Garnish top with perfect California walnut halves.

*Orange Filling:* Cream 1 cup butter. Gradually add 2 cups sifted confectioners' sugar, creaming well. Beat in 2 teaspoons cocoa (regular-type, dry), ½ teaspoon instant coffee powder, 2 tablespoons *each* cold water and orange juice.

*Mocha Frosting:* Mix 2 cups sifted confectioners' sugar, 2 teaspoons cocoa (regular-type, dry), and ½ teaspoon instant coffee powder; add 2 tablespoons cold water, 3 tablespoons butter or margarine, melted, and ½ teaspoon vanilla; beat till of spreading consistency.

## MOCHA NUT TORTE

Sift together ½ cup sifted all-purpose flour and 2 teaspoons baking powder; stir in 2 cups fine graham-cracker crumbs. Cream ½ cup shortening and 1 cup sugar thoroughly; add 3 egg yolks and 1 teaspoon vanilla; beat till light.

Dissolve 1 tablespoon instant coffee powder in 1 cup cold water. Add flour mixture to creamed mixture alternately with coffee, beating till smooth. Stir in ¾ cup chopped California walnuts. Fold in 3 stiff-beaten egg whites.

Bake in 2 paper-lined 8x1½-inch round pans at 375° for 35 minutes. Cool in pans. Remove from pans; peel off paper; split each layer. Spread Filling between layers and on top of each layer. Trim top with chocolate curls. Chill.

*Filling:* Prepare one 3¾- or 3⅝-ounce package *instant* vanilla pudding mix according to the package directions *using only* 1¼ cups milk. Add 1 teaspoon instant coffee powder and chill. Fold in ½ cup whipping cream, whipped.

Almond-brittle Torte—a dessert spectacular. The airy sponge cake is covered lavishly with whipped cream and coffee candy, then studded with toasted almond halves.

## ALMOND-BRITTLE TORTE

### Sponge Cake:

Sift 1½ cups sifted all-purpose flour and ¾ cup sugar into mixing bowl. Make well in center; add ½ cup (8) egg yolks, ¼ cup cold water, 1 tablespoon lemon juice, and 1 teaspoon vanilla. Beat till batter is smooth.

Beat 1 cup (8) egg whites with 1 teaspoon cream of tartar and 1 teaspoon salt till very soft peaks form; add ¾ cup sugar gradually, two tablespoons at a time; continue beating till stiff peaks form. Fold egg yolk batter gently into egg white meringue.

Pour batter into *ungreased* 10-inch tube pan. Carefully cut through batter, going around tube 5 or 6 times with knife to break large air bubbles. Bake in moderate oven (350°) about 50 to 55 minutes or till top springs back when touched lightly. Invert pan; cool. Remove cake.

Split crosswise in 4 equal layers. Assemble torte with whipped cream and Almond-brittle topping as directed.

### Almond-brittle Topping:

¾ cup sugar
½ teaspoon instant coffee powder
2 tablespoons light corn syrup
2 tablespoons water
1½ teaspoons *sifted* soda

While cake bakes, fix candy part of topping: In saucepan, mix first 4 ingredients. Cook to soft-crack stage (285° to 290°). Remove from heat; add soda at once. Stir vigorously, but only till mixture blends and pulls away from sides of pan. Quickly pour into buttered 8x8x2-inch pan. *Do not spread or stir.* Cool. Tap bottom of pan to remove candy. Crush into coarse crumbs.

When cake is thoroughly cool, whip 2 cups whipping cream with 1 tablespoon sugar and 2 teaspoons vanilla.

Spread half the whipped cream between cake layers and the remainder over top and sides. Cover with candy crumbs, trim with ½ cup toasted almond halves inserted into frosting porcupine-style all over cake.

# FESTIVE FRUITCAKES

## GOLDEN FRUITCAKE

Cut 1 cup dried apricots in thin slices; cover with boiling water; let stand 20 minutes; drain. Combine with 2 cups *each* chopped candied pineapple and golden raisins; 1 cup *each* dark raisins, halved candied cherries, chopped citron, and chopped candied orange peel; ½ cup chopped candied lemon peel, 2 cups chopped pecans, and 1 cup slivered almonds.

Cream 1¼ cups shortening, 1½ cups honey, and 2 teaspoons rum extract *or* vanilla till light; beat in 6 eggs. Sift together 2½ cups sifted all-purpose flour, 1¼ teaspoons salt, 1 teaspoon baking powder, 1 teaspoon cinnamon, ½ teaspoon nutmeg, and ¼ teaspoon cloves. Add to creamed mixture, mixing to smooth batter. Fold in fruit and nut mixture.

Turn into greased and foil-lined pans: two 11x4x3-inch fruitcake pans and one 5½x3x2¼-inch pan *or* one 10-inch tube pan and one 7½x 3¾x2¼-inch loaf pan. Bake at 275° about 2 hours for loaves, 3 hours for tube pan. (Place shallow pan of hot water on bottom of oven.) Cool; remove from pans. Wrap in fruit-juice-soaked cloth and foil. Store in a cool place for several weeks. Makes 7 pounds fruitcake.

Fruitcake and coffee make a gracious welcome for holiday guests. Golden Fruitcake is decked with pecan halves and holly sprigs.

## LIGHT FRUITCAKE

¾ pound (1½ cups) candied cherries, chopped
1 cup light raisins
½ pound (1 cup) candied pineapple, chopped
¼ pound (½ cup) mixed chopped candied fruits and peels
¼ pound (½ cup) candied lemon peel, chopped
¼ pound (½ cup) candied orange peel, chopped
1 cup California walnuts, chopped
3 cups sifted all-purpose flour
1 cup butter or margarine
1 cup sugar
4 eggs
¼ cup light corn syrup
¼ cup orange juice
¼ cup sherry

Combine chopped fruits, peels, and nuts; mix with *1 cup* of the flour. Cream butter and sugar till light; add eggs, one at a time, beating well after each. Combine corn syrup, orange juice, and sherry; add alternately with remaining flour to creamed mixture. Fold in fruits and nuts. Pour into two well-greased 5½-cup ring molds. Bake at 275° for 1 hour and 15 minutes. Makes two 2-pound 4-ounce cakes.

Or pour batter into 8 well-greased 4½x2¾x 2¼-inch pans. Bake at 275° about 1 hour.

For individual cakes, pour batter into foil muffin cups, using ¼ cup batter for each cup. Bake at 275° about 45 minutes. Makes 2½ dozen.

## FRUITCAKE POINTERS

Plan to chop fruits and nuts one day, finish and bake cake the next for easy preparation.

Cool fruitcakes in pans, then turn out.

Wrap cakes in brandy-, wine-, or juice-soaked cloth, then in foil. Moisten again once a week. Store cakes in foil, clear plastic wrap, or airtight container. Keep in cool place.

Chill before slicing, for thin, perfect slices.

For best flavor (blended and mellow), make holiday fruitcakes 3 to 4 weeks ahead.

Groom's cake is an often neglected tradition. This is the cake, taken home and tucked under a pillow, that brings dreams of the future. Make it of Dark Fruitcake. Cut in tiny pieces, boxed and beribboned, it can be given to each departing wedding guest.

## DARK FRUITCAKE

Combine one 6-ounce can frozen orange juice concentrate, thawed, with ½ cup molasses and one 15-ounce package (3 cups) raisins in saucepan. Cook over medium heat, stirring occasionally till mixture comes to a boil. Reduce heat and simmer 5 minutes. Remove from heat. Stir in one 1-pound jar (2 cups) mixed chopped candied fruits and peels.

Cream ½ cup butter or margarine and ⅔ cup sugar. Blend in 3 eggs, one at a time. Sift together 1¼ cups sifted all-purpose flour, ⅛ teaspoon soda, 1 teaspoon cinnamon, ½ teaspoon nutmeg, ¼ teaspoon allspice, and ¼ teaspoon cloves. Stir into creamed mixture. Stir in fruit and peel mixture and ½ cup chopped California walnuts; mix well till all fruit is coated.

Line one 11x4x3-inch pan and two 5½x3x 2¼-inch pans with heavy paper, allowing ½ inch to extend above all sides. Pour batter into pans, filling about ¾ full. Bake in very slow oven (275°) about 2¼ to 2½ hours for large loaf and about 1½ hours for smaller loaves. Cool cakes in pans; remove. Wrap in foil or clear plastic wrap and store in cool place several weeks. Makes about 3½ pounds fruitcake.

## CHOCOLATE FRUITCAKE

*Festive surprise! Good with hot coffee after caroling—*

½ cup shortening
1 cup sugar
3 eggs
3 1-ounce squares unsweetened chocolate, melted
2 cups sifted all-purpose flour
2 teaspoons baking powder
1 teaspoon salt
1 teaspoon cinnamon
⅓ cup milk
3 cups mixed chopped candied fruits and peels
1 cup raisins
1 cup broken California walnuts

Cream shortening and sugar till light. Add eggs, one at a time, beating well. Stir in chocolate. Sift together dry ingredients; add to creamed mixture alternately with milk. Stir in fruits and nuts. Turn into greased, paper-lined 10-inch tube pan. Bake at 275° for 1 hour and 45 minutes or till done. Cool; remove from pan. Wrap in foil; store in cool place several weeks.

Decorated fruitcakes are thoughtful gifts for friends and neighbors. Brush with hot corn syrup and trim with candied cherries, nuts, gumdrops, or marzipan fruits. When set, brush with a second coat of glaze. Allow the glaze to dry before wrapping.

# NEW TRICKS WITH CAKE MIXES

## LEMON POUND CAKE

4 eggs
1 package 2-layer-size yellow cake mix
1 3¾- or 3⅝-ounce package *instant* lemon pudding mix (dry)
¾ cup water
⅓ cup salad oil
Lemon Glaze

Beat eggs till thick and lemon-colored. Add cake mix, pudding mix, water, and oil; beat 10 minutes at medium speed on electric mixer. Pour into ungreased 10-inch tube pan with removable bottom. Bake at 350° about 50 minutes. *Leaving cake on pan bottom*, remove sides of pan from hot cake. Using 2-tined fork, prick holes in top of cake. Drizzle Lemon Glaze over top and spread on sides of cake. Cool completely; remove pan bottom. Garnish with *thin* slices of lemon.

*Lemon Glaze:* Heat 2 cups sifted confectioners' sugar and ⅓ cup lemon juice to boiling.

## PINEAPPLE DELIGHT CAKE

1 package 1-layer-size yellow cake mix
1 1-pound 6-ounce can pineapple pie filling
3 egg whites
6 tablespoons sugar
2 tablespoons flaked coconut

Prepare cake mix according to package directions. Bake in greased and lightly floured 8x1½-inch round pan in moderate oven (350°) 25 minutes. Cool. Split to form 2 layers. Spread *half* the pie filling on bottom layer; replace top. Spread remaining filling on top of cake to within ½-inch of edge. Beat egg whites to soft peaks; gradually add sugar, beating to stiff peaks. Spread over top and sides of cake. Sprinkle coconut over top. Bake at 350° for 10 minutes or till lightly browned. Cool.

Popular quick-and-easy Lemon Pound Cake is double lemon flavored with a lemon pudding mix and zesty lemon glaze.

## PINK LEMONADE CAKE

*A perfect party cake!*—

1 package 2-layer-size yellow cake mix
1 quart vanilla ice cream
1 6-ounce can frozen pink lemonade concentrate, thawed
5 or 6 drops red food coloring

• • •

1 cup whipping cream
2 tablespoons sugar

Prepare cake mix according to package directions. Bake in two 9x1½-inch round cake pans; remove from pans and cool. Meanwhile, stir ice cream to soften and quickly stir in ⅓ cup of the lemonade concentrate and food coloring. Spread evenly in foil-lined 9x1½-inch round cake pan. Freeze 2 or 3 hours or till firm.

Place cake layer on serving plate; top with ice cream layer, then with second cake layer. Whip cream with remaining concentrate and 2 tablespoons sugar till stiff. Frost sides and top of cake; return to freezer at least 1 hour.

## BROILED PARTY CAKE

*Cake from a mix frosted with a melt-in-the-mouth mixture of apricot preserves, marshmallows, and coconut— then broiled to golden perfection—*

1 package 2-layer-size yellow cake mix
1 12-ounce jar (1 cup) apricot preserves
1 tablespoon lemon juice
1 3½-ounce can (1⅓ cups) flaked coconut
1½ cups miniature marshmallows

Prepare cake mix according to package directions. Bake in greased and floured 13x9x2-inch pan in moderate oven (350°) about 35 minutes. Combine apricot preserves and lemon juice; stir in coconut and marshmallows. Spread evenly over top of hot cake. Broil 3 to 4 inches from heat about 1 minute or till marshmallows are golden brown. Cool before serving.

## BERRY MERINGUE CAKE

1 package 2-layer-size yellow cake mix
1⅓ cups orange juice
4 egg yolks
1½ teaspoons grated orange peel
4 egg whites
¼ teaspoon cream of tartar
1 cup sugar
1 pint fresh strawberries
2 tablespoons sugar
1 cup whipping cream

Combine first 4 ingredients; beat 4 minutes at medium speed on electric mixer. Pour into 2 greased and floured 9x1½-inch round pans. Beat egg whites with cream of tartar to soft peaks; gradually add 1 cup sugar, beating to stiff peaks. Spread evenly over batter. Bake at 350° for 35 minutes; cool.

Remove from pans, meringue side up. Mash ½ cup strawberries with 2 tablespoons sugar; add whipping cream; whip till stiff. Spread ⅔ of cream mixture over bottom layer. Reserving a few whole berries, slice remainder; place over cream mixture. Add top layer; top with remaining cream and reserved berries.

## PLYMOUTH CRANBERRY CAKE

1 1-pound can (2 cups) whole cranberry
   sauce
2 tablespoons butter or margarine
1 package 1-layer-size white cake mix
¼ cup butter or margarine
½ cup sifted confectioners' sugar
½ cup cold water
1½ teaspoons cornstarch
½ teaspoon vinegar
1 teaspoon vanilla

Break up cranberry sauce in buttered 8¼x1¾-inch round ovenware cake dish, spreading evenly. Dot with 2 tablespoons butter. Prepare cake mix according to package directions; pour over cranberries. Bake at 350° for 35 to 40 minutes. Let stand 10 minutes; invert on plate. Serve warm with *Butter Sauce:* Cream ¼ cup butter. Gradually add confectioners' sugar, creaming till fluffy. In small saucepan, combine cold water and cornstarch; cook and stir till thick and clear. Stir hot mixture into butter mixture. Add vinegar and vanilla. Serve warm over cake.

Springtime captured in a cake! Both Easy Daffodil Cake and its fluffy lemon-spiked frosting are high, light, and handsome.

## EASY DAFFODIL CAKE

Prepare 1 package angel cake mix according to package directions; divide batter in half. Combine ¼ teaspoon yellow food coloring and 1 teaspoon water; fold into *half* the batter. Spoon batters alternately into ungreased 10-inch tube pan. Bake as directed on package. Invert; cool.

Frost with *Lemon Frosting:* Combine 2 egg whites, 2 tablespoons lemon juice, 1 cup sugar, ¼ teaspoon cream of tartar, and dash salt in top of double boiler; beat 1 minute with electric or rotary beater. Cook over boiling water, beating to stiff peaks. Fold in 1 cup miniature marshmallows and ½ teaspoon grated lemon peel.

## RHUBARB MALLOW CAKE

Spoon one 12-ounce package frozen rhubarb, thawed, into greased, waxed paper-lined 8x8x2-inch pan. Sprinkle with 1½ cups miniature marshmallows and ¼ cup brown sugar. Prepare 1 package 1-layer-size yellow cake mix according to package directions. Spread over topping. Bake at 350° for 40 to 45 minutes. Cool 5 minutes; invert on plate; remove paper. Serve warm.

# ORANGE HONEY CAKE

Combine 1 package 2-layer-size yellow cake mix, 1¼ cups water, 2 eggs, ¼ cup honey, and 1 teaspoon grated orange peel; beat 3 minutes. Bake in 2 greased and lightly floured 9x1½-inch round pans in moderate oven (350°) 30 to 35 minutes. Frost with Orange Butter Frosting.

*Orange Butter Frosting:* Cream ¼ cup butter or margarine; gradually add 2 cups sifted confectioners' sugar and blend well. Gradually add an additional 2 cups sifted confectioners' sugar. Add enough fresh orange juice to make of spreading consistency (about ¼ cup); beat well.

# CARAMEL-TOPPED CAKE

Prepare 1 package 1-layer-size yellow cake mix according to package directions. Pour into greased 9x9x2-inch pan. Bake in moderate oven (350°) 25 to 30 minutes or till done. In small saucepan, combine ¾ cup brown sugar, ½ cup quick-cooking rolled oats, ¼ cup butter, and ¼ cup milk; bring to boil. Pour over cake. Return to oven for about 5 minutes or till bubbly.

# RIBBON CAKE

*Try this one for your next birthday party. Youngsters love the multicolored layers—*

1 package 1-layer-size white cake mix
2 drops red food coloring
1 package 1-layer-size yellow cake mix
1 1-ounce square unsweetened chocolate, melted and cooled
1 tablespoon milk
5 drops yellow food coloring

Prepare white cake mix according to package directions; divide batter in half. To *one half* add red food coloring; leave other portion white. Pour each batter into paper-lined 8x1½-inch round cake pan. Bake in moderate oven (350°) 12 to 15 minutes or till done. Prepare yellow cake mix according to package directions; divide batter in half. To *one half* add the chocolate and milk. Add yellow food coloring to other half. Pour each batter into paper-lined 8x1½-inch round cake pan. Bake in moderate oven (350°) 12 to 15 minutes or till done. Cool. Fill and frost with Seven Minute Frosting.

# PEACH COCONUT TORTE

Drain one 1-pound 14-ounce can (3½ cups) peach halves, reserving 3 tablespoons syrup. Melt 3 tablespoons butter or margarine in a saucepan; add reserved syrup and ⅓ cup brown sugar. Pour into 5-cup ring mold. Sprinkle ⅔ cup flaked coconut over mixture.

Prepare 1 package 1-layer-size white cake mix according to package directions; spoon over coconut. Bake in moderate oven (350°) 25 to 30 minutes or till done. Cool 1 minute; invert on plate. Pile peach halves in center. Spoon peach sundae topping from jar over peaches. Serve cake while warm.

# CHOCOLATE CHIP CAKE

Prepare 1 package 2-layer-size white cake mix according to package directions. Reserving 3 tablespoons chocolate pieces, chop remainder of one 6-ounce package (1 cup) semisweet chocolate pieces. In 2 greased and lightly floured 8x1½- or 9x1½-inch round pans, alternate layers of batter with chopped chocolate. Bake as directed on package. When cool, frost with Sea Foam Frosting. Dot with reserved chocolate.

# HOLIDAY FRUITCAKE

1 package 2-layer-size white cake mix
4 eggs
¼ cup water
2 teaspoons salt
2 teaspoons lemon extract

• • •

½ cup sifted all-purpose flour
1 pound pecan halves
½ pound candied cherries
½ pound candied pineapple, cut up
1 pound light raisins

Combine cake mix, *1 egg*, water, salt, and lemon extract; beat till smooth. Add remaining eggs, one at a time, beating well after each. Sift flour over fruits and nuts; mix well and stir into batter. Line 10-inch tube pan (with removable bottom) with foil. Fill with batter; press down. Bake in very slow oven (275°) for 2½ to 3 hours or till done. (Place shallow pan of hot water on bottom of oven during baking.) Cool; remove cake from pan. If desired, glaze and trim with candied fruit. Makes 4½ pounds fruitcake.

## QUICK BLITZ TORTE

*Mocha layers are topped with a baked-on meringue made from a frosting mix. Great idea—great dessert—*

  1 package 2-layer-size chocolate cake mix
  1 tablespoon instant coffee powder
  1 package fluffy white frosting mix
  ⅔ cup slivered almonds
  1 2-ounce package dessert topping mix

Prepare cake mix according to package directions; add instant coffee powder to dry ingredients. Pour into 2 greased and lightly floured 9x1½-inch round cake pans. Bake in moderate oven (350°) 20 minutes.

Meanwhile, prepare frosting mix according to package directions. Remove cake layers from oven; quickly spread frosting over tops, keeping it from touching cake pans. Sprinkle each layer with half the almonds. Return to oven and bake 15 minutes more. Cool layers in pans. (The frosting will settle somewhat as cake cools.) Remove cake from pans.

Prepare dessert topping mix according to package directions. Place one cake layer on plate, frosting side up; spread with whipped topping. Top with second layer. Chill.

## SPICY PUMPKIN CAKE

*A cake with the smooth, spicy flavor of pumpkin pie. The whipped cream topping is a perfect partner—*

  1 package 2-layer-size spice cake mix
  ½ teaspoon soda
  1 cup milk
  1 cup canned pumpkin
  ½ cup chopped California walnuts
  ½ cup dates, finely cut
  1 cup whipping cream
  2 tablespoons honey
  ¼ teaspoon cinnamon

Combine cake mix and soda; proceed according to package directions substituting milk for the first addition of liquid and pumpkin for the second addition. Fold in nuts and dates. Bake in 2 greased and lightly floured 9x1½-inch round pans according to package directions. Cool; remove from pans. Cool completely.

Whip cream with honey and cinnamon. Spread between layers and on top of cake. Chill.

## UPSIDE-DOWN APPLE CAKE

  3 medium tart apples, pared, cored, and sliced very thin
  1 cup apple juice
  ⅓ cup butter or margarine
  1 cup brown sugar
  1 package 2-layer-size spice cake mix
  Maraschino cherry halves
  ½ cup chopped California walnuts

Simmer apple slices in apple juice till tender, about 5 minutes. Drain, reserving juice. In 13x9x2-inch pan, combine ¼ *cup* reserved hot apple juice, butter, and brown sugar. Place pan in oven till butter melts.

Prepare spice cake mix according to package directions, using remaining reserved apple juice as part of liquid. Arrange apple slices and several maraschino cherry halves in brown sugar mixture; sprinkle with nuts. Spoon batter into pan. Bake in moderate oven (350°) about 45 minutes or till done. Cool 1 to 2 minutes; invert on serving plate. Serve warm.

## TOMATO SOUP SPICE CAKE

Prepare 1 package 2-layer-size spice cake mix according to package directions using one 10¾-ounce can condensed tomato soup and ¼ cup water as liquid. Add ½ cup *each* raisins and chopped nuts. Bake in 2 greased and lightly floured 8x1½-inch round pans in moderate oven (350°) 30 to 35 minutes or till done. Cool 10 minutes; remove from pans. Cool and frost with Golden Butter Frosting.

## MOCHA MYSTERY DELIGHT

  1 package 1-layer-size chocolate cake mix
  1 tablespoon instant coffee powder
  2½ cups cold water
  1 4-ounce package *regular* chocolate pudding mix

Prepare cake mix according to package directions. Turn batter into greased and floured 9x9x2-inch baking pan. Stir instant coffee powder into water; gradually add to pudding mix; blend well. Pour evenly over cake batter. Bake in moderate oven (350°) about 45 minutes or till done. Serve warm with whipped cream.

Company-fare Mocha Torte can be chilled overnight, to avoid day-of-the-party preparation. No one will ever know this scrumptious dessert is so easy to make!

## DEVILICIOUS CHERRY CAKE

   1 package 2-layer-size devil's food
      cake mix
   1 1-pound can pitted dark sweet cherries
   ¼ cup sugar
   2 tablespoons cornstarch
   ¼ cup Burgundy wine
   1 8-ounce package cream cheese, softened
   ¼ cup sugar
   2 tablespoons milk
   ¼ teaspoon vanilla

Prepare cake mix according to package directions. Bake in a 13x9x2-inch baking pan. Cool.

Drain cherries, reserving syrup. In saucepan, blend ¼ cup sugar and cornstarch; gradually add cherry syrup, mixing well. Cook and stir over medium heat till mixture thickens and boils. Remove from heat; stir in wine and cherries.

Beat cream cheese, ¼ cup sugar, milk, and vanilla till fluffy. Cut cake into squares. Top each square with a small mound of cream cheese mixture; serve warm cherry sauce over all.

## MOCHA TORTE

   1 package 2-layer-size white cake mix
   1 6-ounce package (1 cup) semisweet
      chocolate pieces
   3 cups miniature marshmallows
   ½ cup milk
   2 teaspoons instant coffee powder
   1 cup whipping cream, whipped

Prepare cake mix according to package directions. Bake in greased 13x9x2-inch pan. Cool; remove from pan. Cool completely.

For Mocha Frosting, combine chocolate pieces, marshmallows, milk, and coffee powder in top of double boiler. Heat and stir over hot water till marshmallows melt. Remove from heat; cover and chill. Fold in whipped cream.

Cut cake in half *lengthwise;* with long knife, split each half of cake into 2 layers, using row of toothpicks to guide knife. Spread chilled Mocha Frosting between layers; frost top and sides. Cover and chill for several hours. Slice about 1 inch thick.

## DELLA ROBBIA TORTE

Prepare 1 package lemon chiffon cake mix according to package directions. Grease *bottoms only* of three 9x1½-inch round pans. Divide batter among pans and bake in moderate oven (350°) 30 to 35 minutes. Invert to cool. If desired, using ½ cup white rum, brush tops of cake layers with rum; let stand 20 minutes.

Prepare one 3- or 3¼-ounce package *regular* vanilla pudding mix according to package directions *but using only* 1½ *cups milk.* Add 1 teaspoon vanilla. Cover; chill, stirring once or twice. Beat smooth; fold in 1 cup whipping cream, whipped.

Spread pudding between layers. Melt ½ cup apple jelly; stir in 1 tablespoon lemon juice; cool. Arrange one 8½-ounce can pineapple slices, drained and halved, 5 drained canned pear halves, 5 drained canned apricot halves, and 11 maraschino cherries as shown in photo. Spoon cooled glaze over fruit. Chill 5 to 6 hours.

## PINK AND WHITE MARBLE CAKE

Prepare 1 package angel cake mix using package directions. Tint ⅓ of batter pink with several drops red food coloring and add ¼ teaspoon peppermint extract. Spoon pink and white batters alternately into ungreased 10-inch tube pan. Bake as directed on package. Invert; cool. Prepare 1 package fluffy white frosting mix according to package directions; tint pink with red food coloring. Frost cake.

## CHOCOLATE RIPPLE CAKE

Prepare 1 package angel cake mix according to package directions. Combine ⅓ cup instant cocoa (dry) and one 3½-ounce can (1⅓ cups) flaked coconut. Place ⅓ of cake batter in 10-inch tube pan; top with ½ the coconut mixture. Repeat and top with remaining cake batter. Bake according to package directions.

Della Robbia Torte is prepared from a cake mix, pudding mix, canned fruit, and jelly glaze—what could be simpler yet still look as though it took hours of preparation.

# BERRY CLOUD DESSERT

1 package angel cake mix
2 egg whites
⅔ cup sugar
1 cup fresh whole strawberries,
   slightly mashed
Dash salt

Prepare and bake cake mix according to package directions. Combine egg whites and remaining ingredients in mixing bowl. Beat at low speed on electric mixer till blended. Gradually increase to high speed and beat 5 to 6 minutes or until stiff peaks form. Frost top and sides of cake with mixture.

*Note:* If desired, use one 10-ounce package frozen strawberries, partially thawed, and reduce sugar to ½ cup.

# COFFEE-DATE SPONGE CAKE

1 package orange chiffon cake mix
2 cups whipping cream
⅔ cup sugar
2 tablespoons instant coffee powder
¾ cup chopped pitted dates

Prepare cake mix according to package directions; bake in tube pan; cool. Split into 3 layers. Whip cream with sugar and instant coffee powder till fluffy; spread over the two lower layers. Sprinkle dates over whipped cream. Stack layers and cover top and sides with remaining whipped cream. Garnish top with whole dates.

# NEAPOLITAN CAKE

1 package angel cake mix
½ gallon Neapolitan ice cream
1 4-ounce package dessert topping mix

Prepare and bake cake mix according to package directions; cool inverted. Let ice cream soften at room temperature about 10 to 15 minutes. Slice cake into 4 layers. With sharp, long-bladed knife, cut ice cream into layers according to flavor. Spread chocolate ice cream on bottom cake layer, vanilla on second layer, and strawberry on third layer. Stack on serving plate; replace top cake layer. Place in freezer. Prepare topping mix. Remove cake from freezer; frost with topping. Freeze 2 to 3 hours.

# CRUNCHY APRICOT CAKE

1 1-pound 6-ounce can apricot pie filling
1 package 1-layer-size white cake mix
1 egg
½ cup flaked coconut
½ cup chopped pecans
½ cup butter or margarine, melted

Spread pie filling in bottom of 9x9x2-inch baking dish. Combine cake mix, ⅓ cup water, and egg. Beat 4 minutes at medium speed on electric mixer. Pour over pie filling; sprinkle with coconut and pecans. Drizzle melted butter or margarine over top. Bake in moderate oven (350°) for 40 minutes. Serve warm.

# PEANUT BUTTER QUICK CAKE

1 package 2-layer-size yellow cake mix
⅛ cup peanut butter
⅛ cup light cream *or* evaporated milk
1½ cups brown sugar
1 cup flaked coconut

Prepare cake mix according to package directions. Bake in a 13x9x2-inch baking pan; cool 5 minutes. Meanwhile combine peanut butter, cream, and brown sugar in saucepan; cook and stir till mixture is boiling. Spread over cake; broil about 4 inches from heat 2 to 3 minutes or till frosting is bubbly. Top with coconut; broil just till coconut is toasted.

# GINGERSCOTCH CAKE

1 package 2-layer-size butterscotch
   cake mix
½ cup chopped California walnuts
2 tablespoons chopped candied ginger
1 1-ounce square semisweet chocolate,
   grated

Prepare cake mix according to package directions. Stir in nuts, ginger, and chocolate. Bake in 2 greased and lightly floured 8x1½-inch round cake pans in moderate oven (350°) about 35 minutes. Cool 10 minutes; remove from pan. Serve with whipped cream.

*Note:* Or, bake batter in a greased and lightly floured 13x9x2-inch baking pan for 40 minutes, or till cake tests done.

78

# CAKE CUES

Always let melted chocolate cool slightly before blending into the creamed mixture. Scrape the sides of bowl frequently with rubber spatula.

To fold stiff-beaten egg whites into batter, use rubber spatula with down-up-over motion; turn bowl as you work. Fold gently; don't stir.

For a shortening-type cake, grease and lightly flour pans, or line bottoms with waxed or baking pan liner paper. Push batter to sides of pan.

 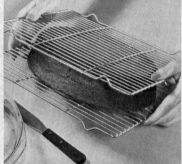 

When baking two layers, place pans as shown. Don't let them touch oven walls or each other. With more layers, stagger pans on two racks.

Cool cake in pan about 10 minutes; loosen edges. Place inverted rack on cake; turn all over; lift off pan. Put second rack over cake. Turn.

Turn angel or chiffon cakes upside down as they come from oven till cool to keep from falling. A pop bottle makes a stand for tube pan.

In these recipes, regular-type all-purpose flour is used unless cake flour is specified. Recipes also use double-acting baking powder.

Be sure to use fresh eggs. Eggs will separate more easily when cold, but the whites will whip up better if at room temperature.

To prepare sour milk, add enough sweet milk to 1 tablespoon lemon juice or vinegar to make 1 cup liquid. Let stand 5 minutes.

Cake is done when it shrinks slightly from sides of pan, springs back when pressed lightly with finger, or when a cake tester or toothpick inserted in center of cake comes out clean.

When adding dry ingredients alternately with liquid, begin and end with the dry ingredients, beating just till smooth after each addition.

An electric mixer makes for easier and better creaming and beating, but a good job can also be done with vigorous beating by hand.

Careful measuring assures correct proportion. Insufficient creaming of shortening and sugar may cause a coarse-grained cake. Extreme overbeating may cause tunneling or a heavy, compact texture. Use correct size and type of pan.

Check accuracy of oven regulator occasionally—too slow an oven will cause cake to fall.

## FREEZING AND STORAGE HINTS

Cakes may be frozen frosted or unfrosted, but keep longer and better if frozen unfrosted. Butter frostings and the cooked-candy type, such as fudge, freeze well. Soft frostings, boiled icings, and cream fillings are not recommended for freezing.

Set unfrosted cake on foil-covered cardboard. Slip into an airtight plastic bag; close tightly. Freeze frosted cake before packaging; wrap as above. Place wrapped cake in labeled box. Use frozen angel and sponge cakes within 1 month; other cakes, 4 months; fruitcakes, 1 year. Thaw frosted cakes unwrapped; unfrosted cakes, wrapped.

Store cakes with whipped cream fillings or frostings in refrigerator, other cakes in a cake keeper having a roomy cover.

## PACKING FOR MAILING

Cakes can travel, too. Best travelers are fruitcake, sponge or chiffon cakes, applesauce, date, or other fruit-type cakes. Frost the cake, if you like, using a glaze-type frosting such as confectioners', a butter, or an ornamental icing, or a thick fudge frosting. Avoid fluffy frostings.

If possible, bake cakes in disposable pans and mail pan and all to give cake extra protection. Or wrap in foil or clear plastic wrap and pack in sturdy carton surrounded with 2 inches of cushioning material such as popcorn or crumpled tissue paper.

For a novel cake-by-mail, wrap an unfrosted angel cake in clear plastic wrap; tuck in a can of frosting (that needs no refrigeration) and plastic bags of nuts or candy for trim. Let receiver assemble cake.

## HIGH-ALTITUDE CHANGES

If you live in a high altitude area (3,000 feet above sea level or above), you may find that many cakes will tend to fall and give unpredictable results. This general guide will help you make adjustments in the ingredient proportions. Since each recipe is different, you may have to experiment a few times with each recipe to discover the best proportions. Where two amounts appear, try smaller amount first. Adjust if necessary.

|  | 3,000 feet | 5,000 feet | 7,000 feet |
|---|---|---|---|
| Liquid: add for each cup | 1 to 2 tablespoons | 2 to 4 tablespoons | 3 to 4 tablespoons |
| Baking powder: decrease for each teaspoon | ⅛ teaspoon | ⅛ to ¼ teaspoon | ¼ teaspoon |
| Sugar: decrease for each cup | 0 to 1 tablespoon | 0 to 2 tablespoons | 1 to 3 tablespoons |

# FINISHING TOUCHES

## SEVEN MINUTE FROSTING

*A white frosting to crown your best cake. Try the two variations, too, and please your family three ways—*

2 unbeaten egg whites
1½ cups granulated sugar
2 teaspoons light corn syrup *or*
    ¼ teaspoon cream of tartar
⅓ cup cold water
Dash salt
1 teaspoon vanilla

Place all ingredients except vanilla in top of double boiler (not over heat); beat 1 minute with electric or rotary beater. Place over, but not touching, boiling water and cook, beating constantly, till frosting forms stiff peaks, about 7 minutes (don't overcook).

Remove from boiling water. Pour into mixing bowl, if you wish. Add vanilla and beat till of spreading consistency, about 2 minutes. Frosts tops and sides of two 8- or 9-inch layers, top of 13x9-inch cake, or 2 dozen cupcakes.

## SEA FOAM FROSTING

Prepare Seven Minute Frosting, substituting 1½ cups brown sugar for the granulated sugar.

## BURNT-SUGAR FROSTING

Prepare Seven Minute Frosting, using 1¼ cups granulated sugar, ¼ cup cold water, and substituting 3 to 4 tablespoons cooled Burnt-sugar Syrup* for the corn syrup.

*Use syrup prepared for Burnt-sugar Cake, (see Index) *or* melt (caramelize) ⅓ cup granulated sugar in small, heavy saucepan, stirring constantly. When a deep golden brown syrup, remove from heat and slowly add ⅓ cup boiling water. Heat and stir till all dissolves. Boil to reduce syrup to ¼ cup. Set aside to cool.

**Paired to perfection—Burnt-sugar Cake and Burnt-sugar Frosting are made the old-fashioned way. Caramelized sugar syrup gives sweet-bitter flavor and tempting color.**

## PEPPERMINT FROSTING

Blend together two 3-ounce packages softened cream cheese, 2 tablespoons milk, and dash salt. Gradually add 5 cups sifted confectioners' sugar, beating well after each addition. Stir in ⅓ to ½ cup crushed peppermint-stick candy. Frosts 10-inch tube cake or generously frosts tops and sides of two 8- or 9-inch layers. Decorate with candy canes or crushed candy.

## CREAMY WHITE FROSTING

Blend ½ cup milk and 1 tablespoon cornstarch. Cook and stir over low heat till mixture thickens and boils. Cool. Cream ½ cup shortening and 1 cup sifted confectioners' sugar till fluffy. Beat in cornstarch mixture, ½ teaspoon salt, and 1½ teaspoons vanilla. Add 1½ cups sifted confectioners' sugar, beating smooth. Frosts tops and sides of two 8- or 9-inch layers.

## PINEAPPLE TOPPER

*A broiled-on frosting with tropical accent—*

¼ cup butter or margarine
1 cup brown sugar
1 3½-ounce can (1⅓ cups) flaked coconut
½ cup chopped California walnuts
1 8¾-ounce can (1 cup) crushed
    pineapple, drained

Melt butter; blend in remaining ingredients. Spread on hot or cool 13x9-inch cake. Broil about 3 inches from the heat for 2 minutes or till frosting is bubbly and browned.

## PENUCHE FROSTING

Melt ½ cup butter or margarine; add 1 cup brown sugar. Bring to boiling; cook and stir 1 minute or till slightly thick. Cool 15 minutes. Add ¼ cup hot milk and beat smooth. Beat in 3¼ cups sifted confectioners' sugar till of spreading consistency. Makes enough frosting for tops and sides of two 8- or 9-inch cake layers.

# FLUFFY WHITE FROSTING

*An easy version of Seven Minute Frosting—*

1 cup granulated sugar
⅓ cup water
¼ teaspoon cream of tartar
Dash salt
2 unbeaten egg whites
1 teaspoon vanilla

Combine sugar, water, cream of tartar, and salt in saucepan. Bring to boiling, stirring till sugar dissolves. Very slowly add to unbeaten egg whites in mixing bowl, beating constantly with electric mixer till stiff peaks form. Beat in vanilla. Frosts tops and sides of two 8- or 9-inch layers, or 10-inch tube cake.

# PINK FROSTING

2 cups granulated sugar
1 cup water
3 tablespoons strawberry-flavored gelatin
½ teaspoon cream of tartar
Dash salt
•  •  •
2 egg whites
1 teaspoon vanilla

Combine sugar, water, gelatin, cream of tartar, and salt. Bring to boiling, stirring till sugar dissolves. Slowly add to unbeaten egg whites, beating constantly with electric mixer at high speed till stiff peaks form. Add vanilla. Frosts tops and sides of two 8- or 9-inch layers.

# GOLDEN BUTTER FROSTING

½ cup butter or margarine, softened
1 egg yolk
2 tablespoons buttermilk *or* milk
½ teaspoon vanilla
3 cups sifted confectioners' sugar

Place ingredients in small mixing bowl in order listed. Blend. Beat at medium speed on electric mixer for 3 minutes. If frosting is soft, beat in a little extra sifted confectioners' sugar to make of spreading consistency. Frosts tops and sides of two 8- or 9-inch layers, top of a 13x9-inch cake, or 2 dozen cupcakes.

# BUTTER MALLOW FROSTING

Combine ⅔ cup milk and ½ pound marshmallows (about 30) in saucepan. Cook and stir over low heat till marshmallows dissolve. Cool to room temperature; stir to blend. Cream ½ cup butter or margarine till light and fluffy. Gradually add cooled marshmallow mixture, beating well. Beat in 1 teaspoon vanilla. Frosts top of 13x9-inch cake or top of 9-inch square cake.

# LEMON BUTTER FROSTING

6 tablespoons butter or margarine
4 cups sifted confectioners' sugar
1 egg yolk
1½ teaspoons vanilla
1 teaspoon grated lemon peel
2 to 3 tablespoons light cream

Cream butter; gradually add *half* the confectioners' sugar, blending well. Beat in egg yolk, vanilla, and lemon peel. Gradually add remaining confectioners' sugar; beat well. Add enough light cream to make of spreading consistency. Frosts tops and sides of two 8- or 9-inch layers.

# ORANGE BUTTER FROSTING

Cream ¼ cup butter or margarine; gradually add 2 cups sifted confectioners' sugar, blending well. Add 2 teaspoons grated orange peel. Stir in 1 tablespoon orange juice or enough to make of spreading consistency; beat smooth. Frosts top of 9-inch square cake or 1 dozen cupcakes.

# MINT FROSTING

*A delicate green color—delicious with chocolate cake—*

½ cup butter or margarine
3 cups sifted confectioners' sugar
Dash salt
¼ cup creme de menthe syrup

Cream butter; gradually add *half* the sugar and the salt, beating well. Gradually add about *half* the syrup; blend well. Blend in remaining sugar and syrup, beating constantly. Frosts tops and sides of two 9-inch layers. Decorate with shaved unsweetened chocolate, if desired.

## CHOCOLATE FROSTING

6 tablespoons butter or margarine
4 cups sifted confectioners' sugar
1 egg yolk
1 1-ounce square unsweetened chocolate,
  melted and cooled
1½ teaspoons vanilla
¼ cup light cream

Cream butter; gradually add *half* the sugar, blending well. Add egg yolk, chocolate, and vanilla. Gradually add remaining sugar; beat well. Add cream to make of spreading consistency. Frosts tops and sides of two 8- or 9-inch layers. Trim cake with nuts, if desired.

## MILK CHOCOLATE FROSTING

1 cup granulated sugar
3 1-ounce squares unsweetened chocolate,
  cut in small pieces
1 6-ounce can (⅔ cup) evaporated milk
Dash salt

Put sugar in blender; cover and blend about 1 minute at high speed. Add chocolate, evaporated milk, and salt; blend at high speed about 3 minutes or till thick, using rubber spatula to scrape sides as necessary when blender is turned off. Frosts tops of two 8-inch layers. (If firmer frosting is desired, chill frosted cake.)

## CHOCO PUDDING FROSTING

1 4-ounce package *regular* dark chocolate
  pudding mix
1¼ cups milk
½ cup butter or margarine
½ cup shortening
1 cup sifted confectioners' sugar
1 teaspoon vanilla
¼ teaspoon salt

Cook pudding according to package directions, *using 1¼ cups milk.* Cover surface of pudding with waxed paper or clear plastic wrap; cool to room temperature.

Cream together butter, shortening, and sugar till light and fluffy; stir in vanilla and salt. Gradually add pudding, beating well. Frosts tops and sides of two 9-inch layers.

Place 3 or 4 strips waxed paper over edges of plate. Pull out after decorating cake.

## SOUR CREAM FROSTING

1 6-ounce package (1 cup) semisweet
  chocolate pieces
¼ cup butter or margarine
½ cup dairy sour cream
1 teaspoon vanilla
¼ teaspoon salt
2½ to 2¾ cups sifted confectioners'
  sugar

Melt chocolate pieces and butter over hot, not boiling, water; remove from hot water and blend in sour cream, vanilla, and salt. Gradually add enough confectioners' sugar to make of spreading consistency; beat well. Frosts tops and sides of two 9-inch layers or 10-inch tube cake.

## FAST FUDGE FROSTING

1 1-pound package confectioners' sugar,
  sifted (about 4 cups)
½ cup cocoa (regular-type, dry)
¼ teaspoon salt
⅛ cup boiling water
⅛ cup butter or margarine, softened
1 teaspoon vanilla

Combine sugar, cocoa, and salt. Add boiling water and butter; blend. Add vanilla. Frosts tops and sides of two 8- or 9-inch layers.

For each perky blossom, cut marshmallow in five slices. Squeeze a point on each petal. Overlap petals and press together. Sprinkle with sugar; dot with slice of red gumdrop.

Flexible "shoestring" licorice makes brands on cowboy's cake. Warm licorice slightly, then cut with kitchen shears. Shape into brands and arrange on top and sides of cake.

# CAKE DECORATING IDEAS

*Sugar Bells:* Thoroughly mix 3 cups granulated sugar and 1 egg white. If too dry, add few drops water. Pack firmly into bell-shaped mold. Stand mold on paper; tap gently; lift off mold. Dry till edges are firm but center is still soft. Scoop out center, leaving ⅛- to ¼-inch shell.

*Crisscross Trim:* Spread a creamy butter frosting over cake. Cover top with parallel lines made by drawing tines of a fork through frosting. At right angles, draw fork through frosting again, leaving a ½-inch space between strokes.

*Tinted Coconut:* Place shredded or flaked coconut in jar with few drops of desired food coloring. Cover jar; shake till uniformly colored.

*Coffee Coconut:* In a pint jar, mix 1½ teaspoons *each* instant coffee powder and water. Add one 3½-ounce can flaked coconut. Cover the jar and shake well. Spread on baking sheet; toast in 300° oven about 20 minutes, stirring occasionally. Sprinkle over fluffy frosting on cake.

*Gumdrop Bow:* Between sheets of waxed paper, roll out two large gumdrops in long strips (have sugar on both sides of candy). Cut strips in half lengthwise and trim to ½ inch wide. For each loop of bow, bring ends of 1 strip together. Arrange 2 loops on frosting. Place a small strip over center to cover "seam." Complete bow by adding 2 strips with ends snipped to points.

*Gumdrop Autumn Leaves:* Between sheets of waxed paper, roll out large gumdrops of fall colors. Cut with tiny leaf-shaped cutter or make leaf pattern of cardboard and cut around it with sharp knife. Arrange on frosted cake.

# CAKE-CUTTING HINTS

To cut a frosted layer cake, use a sharp, thin-bladed knife. Dip blade in warm water or wipe with a damp cloth occasionally to keep free of frosting and crumbs. Insert point of knife; keeping point down and handle up, slice with up-and-down motion, pulling knife toward you.

To cut a foam-type cake, use a cake breaker or knife with serrated blade for high, fluffy wedges. When using cake breaker, press prongs gently through cake—turn handle away from slice till cake separates. If using knife, cut with a gentle back-and-forth motion.

Fruitcakes cut best if refrigerated; use a straight-edged, thin-bladed knife. Dip knife in hot water and cut with slow, sawing motion.

Cover unshelled Brazils with cold water; simmer 3 minutes. Drain. Let stand in cold water 1 minute; drain; shell. Cover nuts with cold water; simmer 3 minutes; drain. Cut paper-thin, lengthwise slices with vegetable parer. Place around candied cherries.

Chocolate curls do make a pretty cake or pie trim. Have one 4-ounce package sweet cooking chocolate at room temperature. Using vegetable parer, carefully shave off thin slices of the chocolate. It will curl as you cut. Chocolate temperature is important; if too cold, the curls will break.

Try a fancy sugar design on spice or chocolate cake or gingerbread. Place a lacy open doily over cake. Sift confectioners' sugar over doily; press it through with back of spoon. Carefully lift off doily. You have a pretty trim without extra calories of frosting.

To make gumdrop rose candleholder, roll 4 large gumdrops into ovals on sugared board. Cut in half crosswise. Fold corner at angle; wind to form center. Press on additional half-ovals, shaping the edges like petals. Trim base and insert wire candle holder in center. Add gumdrop leaves.

For frosting cone, cut a 9x17-inch sheet of silicone baking pan liner paper (buy at food stores). Lay sheet flat on table. Grasp top corners as shown, with right hand inside cone, left hand outside.

Turn right hand corner over, rolling right hand toward you till partial cone is made. Circle right hand with the left, changing left-hand grasp. Move hands back and forth till you have a sharp point.

Hold cone near top with thumb and finger. Snip off tip 1¼ to 2 inches from end. Cut straight across, not at an angle. Drop decorating tube into the cone—¾ of the tube should protrude so frosting can't leak.

Using spatula, fill cone three-quarters full with decorating frosting. To seal the cone, flatten sides above frosting; fold corners in, then fold top flap down, as for a package. Now roll the top over again.

*Use Boiled Frosting to frost cakes. It gives a nice smooth surface. The Butter Cream Frosting is used for decorations made directly on cake—leaves, borders, writing, string-work. Royal Frosting becomes very hard and is ideal for make-ahead decorations.*

## BOILED FROSTING

2 cups granulated sugar
½ cup water
¼ teaspoon cream of tartar
4 egg whites (room temperature)
1 teaspoon vanilla
2 cups sifted confectioners' sugar

Cook first 3 ingredients over low heat, stirring till sugar dissolves. Cover pan 2 or 3 minutes to dissolve sugar crystals on sides of pan. Uncover; cook rapidly without stirring to soft-ball stage (236°); remove from heat at once.

When syrup is almost cooked, beat egg whites on electric mixer to stiff peaks. Pour hot syrup in thin stream over egg whites, beating constantly at high speed. Beat 3 minutes more; add vanilla. Reduce speed; add confectioners' sugar gradually. Beat at high speed till mixture is thick enough to hold a definite point.

While frosting cake, keep bowl covered with damp cloth. Dip spatula in hot water as needed. Frosts tops and sides of three 9-inch layers. *Note:* Leftover frosting may be used for writing, string-work, or borders. For borders, add extra sifted confectioners' sugar to make stiff.

## ROYAL FROSTING

3 egg whites (room temperature)
1 1-pound package sifted confectioners' sugar (about 4 cups)
½ teaspoon cream of tartar
1 teaspoon vanilla

Combine all ingredients. Beat with electric mixer 7 to 10 minutes or till very stiff. Keep frosting covered with damp cloth at all times to prevent crust from forming. Makes 3 cups.

Make flowers on silicone paper or waxed paper. Let dry 8 hours before peeling off paper. Dab a little decorating frosting on bottom of each flower to attach to top or sides of cake. Place some flowers at slight angle.

If Royal Frosting upon standing becomes too "marshmallowy" to go through tube easily, whip again. If frosting has been chilled, bring to room temperature before rewhipping.

## BUTTER CREAM FROSTING

Have ½ cup butter or margarine and ½ cup shortening soft but firm; blend in mixer. Add 1 teaspoon vanilla. Slowly add 3 cups sifted confectioners' sugar; beat well. Makes 2 cups.
*For flowers:* If needed, add a bit more sifted confectioners' sugar. Make flowers on silicone or waxed paper; place on cookie sheet. *Harden in refrigerator or freezer 1 hour.* Transfer to cake with spatula. Work fast to keep flowers cold.

# FROSTING DECORATIONS

**A** *Zigzag border.* Use a No. 30 star tube, or for a broader band, No. 48. Hold cone at a 45° angle to surface. Rest tube lightly on surface and start an even, steady pressure on the cone. As you move along, guide the cone in short, side-to-side movements. Practice on waxed paper or inverted pan.

**B** *Shell border.* Use No. 30 star tube. With cone at a 60° angle to cake, rest tube very gently on surface and begin squeezing. As the shell builds up, lift tube about ¼ inch; ease off on the pressure as you pull down. The shell comes down to a point by stopping all pressure at the end of the shell. Make a continuous line of these.

**C** *Reverse shell border.* Similar to (B), except as the shell builds up, guide the cone to *the right* and ease off the pressure. Guide second shell to *the left* and ease off pressure.

**D** *Puff border.* Use No. 12 plain tube. Hold cone upright, tube resting lightly on surface. Apply pressure and stop, lifting tube up ¼ inch as frosting builds up; repeat.

**E** *Button border.* Use No. 32 star tube. Hold cone upright, tube resting lightly on cake. Apply pressure and make a *slight* swirling motion. Lift tube about ¼ inch from cake. Stop pressure and continue swirl till frosting breaks off neatly.

**F** *String-work border.* With No. 3 plain tube in cone, fill with Butter Cream Frosting, Boiled Frosting, or slightly thinned Royal Frosting. If frosting is too soft, it won't hold together; if too stiff, it won't flow smoothly.

Practice on inverted angel cake pan to perfect the technique. Touch edge of cake with tube and start squeezing with an even pressure—let gravity pull the string of frosting down. Then move the frosting tube over about 1½ inches as you squeeze, letting the frosting string drop down about 1 inch, and touch cake edge again. *Your hand should be at the top of the cake all the time, not following the string.*

Make second row under the first. Bow is a horizontal figure "8" with two short strings attached to complete bow effect.

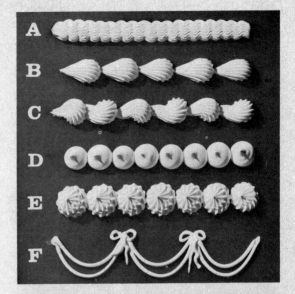

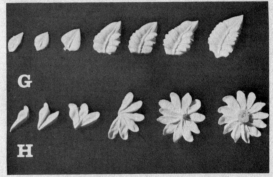

**G** *Leaf.* Use No. 67 leaf tube. Fill frosting cone with Butter Cream Frosting. For plain leaves: With cone at a 45° angle, touch cake with tube and apply light pressure; at halfway point of leaf, stop pressure but move tube along, lifting it up slightly till frosting breaks off.

For ruffly leaves: As you squeeze, move tube back and forth; diminish pressure as you near leaf tip; stop pressure, move out to make fine point.

**H** *Daisy.* Put dot of frosting on "flower nail" and stick a 1½-inch square of waxed paper on top. Then put dot of frosting in center as target. With wide end of No. 103 rose tube touching paper, start at center of nail and squeeze cone, moving to outer edge; ease off pressure. Turn nail; continue petals. Pull paper with daisy off nail. When all daisies are made, dot centers with contrasting colors of frosting.

(A) *Writing.* Use a No. 3 or 4 plain tube. Fill frosting cone with Butter Cream Frosting. Rest tube on surface very lightly. *Relax* and practice with long back-and-forth strokes, using a steady pressure.

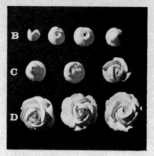

Then try curved letters, guiding the tube with the left forefinger. When writing on the sides of a cake, place the cake at eye level. It is a good idea to practice writing all the words to be used on the cake before you begin on the cake itself. The same tubes and technique can also be used to make simple outline figures of animals or faces for a child's cake. Cake can be placed on a lazy Susan or mixer turntable for ease in turning while decorating.

*Rose.* Use No. 124 rose tube and decorating frosting (stiff enough for petals to stand up). Put waxed or silicone paper on "flower nail". Hold cone at 45° angle, narrow end of tube pointing up and slightly toward center of nail. Squeeze the cone *while turning nail* counterclockwise. Continue till you have a fairly wide base about 1½ inches high (B). Start second dome on top (see first flower, row C). With tube in same position, squeeze 3 slightly overlapping petals around top of dome to make bud (C). The next 5 petals go under bud, standing out a little. For last row, start at bottom of dome, turning tube to side so petals stand out (D).

For birthday, anniversary, or other special occasion, a decorated cake, using party color scheme, is sure to win compliments. Patient practice following directions given on these pages is the key to a professional-looking cake.

# INDEX

# PIES
## A-C

# ADDITIONAL RECIPES

Pages of this final section are for adding recipes from future issues of Better Homes and Gardens magazine and other favorite pies and cakes recipes.